the Waiting Game

THE ESSENTIAL GUIDE
FOR WAIT STAFF

Mike Kirkham,
Peggy Weiss,
and Bill Crawford

TEN SPEED PRESS
Berkeley / Toronto

🖏

Ten Speed Press
P.O. Box 7123
Berkeley, California 94707
www.tenspeed.com

Distributed in Australia by Simon & Schuster Australia, in Canada by Ten Speed Press Canada, in New Zealand by Southern Publishers Group, in South Africa by Real Books, in Southeast Asia by Berkeley Books, and in the United Kingdom and Europe by Airlift Book Company.

Cover and book design by Betsy Stromberg
Copyediting by Carolyn Miller
Illustrations by Missi Jay

Originally published as *The Waiting Game: The Ultimate Guide to Waiting Tables* (Twenty Per Cent Inc., 2000, ISBN 0-9701027-0-4).

Library of Congress Cataloging-in-Publication Data

Kirkham, Mike.
  The waiting game : the essential guide for wait staff / Mike Kirkham, Peggy Weiss, and Bill Crawford.
      p. cm.
Includes index.
  ISBN 1–58008–369–2
  1. Table service. I. Weiss, Peggy. II. Crawford, Bill, 1955– III. Title.
  TX925 .K5697 2002
  642′.6—dc21
                                      2001008410

Printed in the United States

First printing, 2002

1 2 3 4 5 6 7 8 9 10—06 05 04 03 02

CONTENTS

THE WAITING GAME

ACKNOWLEDGMENTS

We would like to thank Dennis Hayes, Brie Mazurek, and all the folks at Ten Speed Press for their confidence in us and their editorial expertise. Missi Jay has been delightful to work with and her illustrations are super. Also, thanks to Ron Weiss and Diana Borden for their patience and encouragement over this past year. Finally, we owe a huge debt of gratitude to the wait staff at Jeffrey's, Shoreline Grill, and Cipollina, and to all our great customers in Austin, Texas, and Washington, D.C.

Foreword

My husband and I love a good meal—especially one served with a smile. Over the years, we have enjoyed eating at numerous restaurants, including Jeffrey's and Shoreline Grill, two of our favorites in Austin. From down-home diners to culinary cafes, we have learned that a good meal is always better with great service.

Many of us can relate to having a bad dining experience. You waited too long for a table. You waited too long for your food. You waited too long for your check. Your food was cold, and your temper was hot. Needless to say, you probably never ate at that restaurant again. George and I are no exception to this experience. Today, our favorite places to eat are those where the house rules are courtesy and timeliness . . . and of course, good food.

The Waiting Game is a guide for learning the art of good service. The authors are experienced restaurateurs and writers who understand American culture. Whether you're just beginning or brushing up on your skills, you'll find what you need to make your guests feel at home as you serve them. The tips and techniques are also great for restaurant owners and managers or for those of you who enjoy entertaining in your own home. Whether you're working at a downtown restaurant or an uptown bistro, good service is always best when it's the specialty of the house.

Laura Bush
Austin, Texas, October 2000

INtRoDUCtioN

We love the restaurant business: It's in our DNA. Between the three of us, we've waited, hosted, tended bar, expedited, cooked, trained, and marketed in over a dozen different restaurants. We've opened restaurants, closed restaurants, and opened more restaurants. Currently, we are owners of five very different restaurants in Austin, Texas, and Washington, D.C. They range from award-winning fine dining to cafeteria-style campus food. What these places have in common is our commitment to offering the guest a great experience. We love to see people enjoying good food, lively conversation, and friendly service. We like knowing that the guests in our restaurants, for that brief time, would rather be there than anywhere else.

For years, we struggled with training our wait staff, using whatever training materials we could find. Although we took training our employees very seriously, we made our share of mistakes in the process. Sometimes our staff meetings turned into rumbling, grumbling complaint sessions, wasting everyone's time. Other times, we found ourselves covering the same information over and over. Then, a few years ago, we decided to take a step back and write down the service standards we expected of our wait staff. We found this detailed manual to be a great training tool for new staff, and a great brush-up course for our seasoned staff. We kept writing and rewriting the material until we realized that we had an informal, practical, compact book: *The Waiting Game*. We found so much demand for the book that we self-published it and offered it to the general public. In the two years that the book has been available, the response has been overwhelmingly positive. Managers have bought the book for their wait staff, and parents have bought the book for their teenaged and young-adult children. Some of our most enthusiastic readers have been people who are not in the restaurant business but who simply enjoy eating out. These people claim that *The Waiting Game* has given them valuable insight into the workings of the restaurant business. After reading our book, they understand what proper service is all about. Some people even use it as a guide for home entertaining.

Playing the Waiting Game

Since we wrote the first edition of *The Waiting Game*, we have led training seminars for a variety of different restaurants and have talked with restaurant managers across the country. Of course, as we met and worked with an assortment of different people in different kinds of restaurants, we learned a great deal of new information about proper service and wait-staff training. This new edition of *The Waiting Game* incorporates that new material as well as the new training techniques we learned working with restaurant staff across the country.

The Waiting Game is an introduction and a general handbook to waiting tables. We intended for this book to be practical and genuinely useful. It is not the definitive word on the subject, as there is a great deal of variation in waiting tables at different restaurants across the country. This book is written primarily for:

- People with no experience, who want to work in the restaurant industry waiting tables

- Experienced wait people who want an easy reference guide to proper table service
- Restaurant managers looking for an effective training tool

If you've had experience in the restaurant business, you know what you're up against. Enjoy the rest of the book. If you've had no experience in the restaurant business, how can you tell if waiting tables is for you? You should carefully weigh the pluses and minuses of playing the waiting game.

PLUSES	**MINUSES**
Constant cash flow	Variable cash flow
Flexible hours	Weekend and evening hours
Good money-making potential	Limited employee benefits
Interaction with interesting people	Having to deal with all kinds of people
Exciting, fun business	High stress
Leaving your stress at work	Legal liability of serving alcohol
Learning about food and wine	Possible high risk for substance abuse

After seriously considering these benefits and drawbacks, you should also keep in mind that this is a great time to join the restaurant industry. Here's why:

- Every year over 800,000 U.S. restaurants produce sales of approximately $336 billion—that's $930 million every day. The restaurant industry is huge, and it's growing fast.
- The restaurant industry employs 10.2 million people. In the next seven years, industry analysts foresee a need for an additional 1.8 million restaurant employees, including half a million more waiters and waitresses. The job market for wait staff is exploding.
- According to a recent survey of restaurants in forty-five cities, more than half of the respondents listed *service* as their top

restaurant complaint. Restaurant owners realize that a good wait staff is the key to profitability. Waiters and waitresses are in high demand—and can demand respect.

- A fast-growing industry, an exploding job market, and an increased focus on the importance of the wait staff means that your chances of winning the waiting game are better than ever. Skilled wait persons today can earn good money and enjoy good working conditions. Some can even get health insurance, paid vacations, retirement plans, and other benefits.

"I've been waiting tables at the same four-star restaurant for over twenty years. I work four evenings a week and figure I gross just over $40,000 a year. And I love the work—my customers and coworkers are family to me."

—JOHNNY, IN AUSTIN

"I'm taking a break from school and studying for the law school admissions test. I support myself by waiting tables at a great restaurant in the city. I also have time to pursue my passion—acting."

—LUKE, IN LOS ANGELES

"When I was in high school, I took a class in food and beverage management. Right away I knew I liked the restaurant business. After being a hostess and waiting tables, I moved into management. This is a perfect career for me."

—SARAH, IN BATON ROUGE

"I've made millions in the software business, but before that, I waited tables for six years. I always make a point of leaving a 25 percent tip."

—RICHARD, IN SEATTLE

"I recently moved to Reno to wait tables in a fine-dining restaurant. Already I'm making over $75,000 a year. I'm getting all my friends to come out here—there's a huge job market."

—KIM, IN RENO

So, do you think you've got what it takes to win the waiting game? If you've got the desire, this book will provide you with the information and skills you need to earn top dollar and high satisfaction from waiting tables.

Waiting tables can be a fun, high-paying job for anyone who knows how to play to win. Skilled wait persons in some cities make as much as $80,000 per year. Wait staff and others in the restaurant industry enjoy a level of job satisfaction that ranks high above people in other professions. And as a wait person you are in control of your own career. If you have an enterprising spirit and you learn the rules of the waiting game presented in this book, you can go as far as you want to in the restaurant business.

Finally, a word about our title, *The Waiting Game*. Waiting tables *is* a game. It is fun, exciting, and challenging. There are rules to the game and rewards for those who play the game well. These rewards include money, job satisfaction, and the development of valuable business skills. Regardless of whether waiting tables is a brief or long-time chapter of your life, you can benefit greatly from playing the waiting game.

✳ STYLES OF SERVICE ✳

We wrote this book for wait staff and wait-staff managers in full-service restaurants. *Full-service* restaurants are restaurants that offer guests waiter staff service and, usually, wine and alcoholic beverage service. Fast-food restaurants, cafeterias, and buffet-style restaurants are not full service. Full-service restaurants offer the best opportunity to earn good tips and to learn the art of good service.

Full-service restaurants offer several different styles of service. The style that we are discussing in this book is called *American service*. Today, most full-service restaurants in the United States offer American service.

In *American service*, the wait person takes food orders from guests at their table. The orders are then prepared in the kitchen, put on plates, and served by the wait person. The wait person collects payment at the table and the guests are expected to tip the wait person.

In *French service*, the wait person takes the order at the table, then brings out a cart and finishes the preparation of the food at the table before serving the food to the guests. French service used to be very popular, but only a few restaurants offer it today.

In *Russian service,* the wait person takes the order, then the chef places the food on large platters in the kitchen. The wait person brings the platters to the table and serves individual portions to each guest. As with French service, only a few restaurants offer Russian service today.

French service

Russian service

CHAPTER 1

UNDERSTANDING THE HOUSE

People in the restaurant business usually refer to a restaurant as *the house*. It makes sense to call it that. When you invite friends to your own apartment or house, you try to make them feel welcome. You try to make sure they have a good time and want to return. You do the same thing at a restaurant. You welcome guests, make sure they have a good time, and hope they return.

In many houses, we learn to live with other people. We rely on them to do certain jobs, tolerate their weird habits, and enjoy their amusing eccentricities. We have our own jobs to do in a house, and if we do them well, the house is a pleasant place to be.

A restaurant works much the same way. Each person there has to perform a job and get along with others.

Job titles and responsibilities differ from restaurant to restaurant, depending on the size and the nature of the restaurant itself. Here's a basic roster of players and how these players relate to you, the wait person.

A restaurant is divided into three sections:

- The *owners* or *chief executive officers* (CEOs)
- The *front of the house* (FOH), or the dining room
- The *back of the house* (BOH), or the kitchen

THE HOUSE

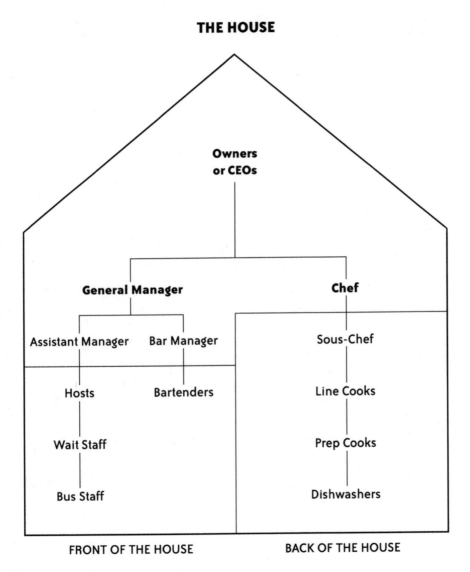

Owners or CEOs

The owners of the restaurant are the financial backers, the people who put up the money for the restaurant. In smaller, independent restaurants, the owner or owners may also work as managers or chefs. In bigger restaurants, you may rarely or never see the owners. It is important to know who the owners are and what they might expect from you if they show up at the restaurant.

The *general manager* runs the house for the owners. If a corporation owns the restaurant, the general manager may also be the CEO of the corporation. As with the owners, it is important to know who the general manager or CEO is and what he or she might expect from you when visiting the restaurant.

the Front of the House

The front of the house (FOH) is commonly known as the dining room. Front-of-the-house employees include managers, wait staff, bar staff, bus staff, and hosts.

Managers

Managers make sure that everything in the restaurant runs smoothly. The manager has to juggle several things at one time, including staff problems and emergencies. This job can be stressful, and managers may sometimes be curt, but remember: The better you get along with your manager, the more you will enjoy your work.

Here are a few things you can do to help your manager:

- Be on time.
- Act professionally.
- Be a team player.
- Leave your personal problems at home.
- Have a positive mental attitude.

In addition to a manager, there may be an assistant manager. Larger restaurants may have a *sommelier* [so-mel-YAY], who is the restaurant's wine specialist; a headwaiter, who is in charge of the dining room or a particular section in the dining room; and a maître d'hôtel, or *maître d'* [may-truh-DEE], who manages the front of the house and supervises the dining room during service. The maître d' knows how to be everywhere at once: greeting guests, sending out complimentary appetizers or desserts, taking wine orders, assisting servers, and thanking guests as they leave.

Hosts

The hosts are responsible for seating the guests. If the restaurant accepts reservations, the hosts must honor the reservations while seating as much walk-in business as possible. They also maintain the waiting list and answer telephone inquiries. Hosts are the first and last people guests see at a restaurant. They must be friendly, helpful, and upbeat. They have to seat guests in such a way that each wait person has an equal amount of business (but not a huge crush!). And they have to give guests seats that please them. This is sometimes an impossible task. You must work with the hosts to maintain a pleasant and inviting atmosphere for the guests.

Wait Staff

This is you! You've got to work with the kitchen and bar staff to place orders and serve the food and beverages to the guests. You have to work with hosts and managers to make sure that guests are seated promptly. You also have to work with bus persons and other wait staff to make sure that tables are cleaned promptly and that all table responsibilities are clear. Teamwork and efficient communication are essential. You're all working together to please the guests. Don't take an "It's not my job" attitude. If the guests aren't pleased, everyone loses.

Bar Staff

All alcoholic beverage service comes through the bar, whether it is a service bar or a dining room bar. The bar manager handles everything related to alcoholic beverages at the house, including ordering, preparing the drink list and sometimes the wine list, and planning drink specials. Many bar managers also have the responsibility of drawing cash to make change for servers and guests. Usually, the bar manager works as a bartender. A bartender should work fast, have a good short-term memory, and have a pleasant disposition. A *bar back* is a bartender's assistant.

Remember, bartenders are usually very social people. When things are slow, chat them up. You need the bartender on your team in order to please your guests. If you spill a drink in the bar area, clean it up. As a wait person, you are generally expected to tip bartenders a percentage of your beverage sales.

Bus Staff

Whether they are called bus staff, bussers, bus persons, or waiter's assistants, these folks are key players on your team. Each restaurant has different duties for their bus staff. These duties include:

- Sorting and polishing silverware
- Folding napkins
- Serving bread and water
- Clearing and resetting the tables
- Helping the wait staff

The bus staff does a hard, physical job. Usually, bus people don't get much reward for their work. Remember that the bus staff is there to help you; they are not your servants or slaves. You should always speak to your bus person with respect. That means "please" and "thank you." Most restaurants require you to tip out your assistant or bus person, and they have guidelines to determine the tip-out. Don't forget to include some verbal gratitude with the cash.

Take care of your bus staff by:

- Helping them bus tables if they fall behind
- *Pre-bussing*, or clearing tables of used silverware and other items as guests finish with them, whenever possible
- Thanking them

The Back of the House

The back of the house (BOH) in a restaurant, also known as the kitchen, is actually a factory. This is where food is prepared and processed for sale. The kitchen is the busiest part of the restaurant, but it is also one of the smallest. Space is always an issue in the kitchen, so watch your step when you're working in the back of the house.

Back-of-the-house employees include the chef, the sous-chef, line cooks, prep cooks, and dishwashers. Cooks are notoriously creative and temperamental. Your job is to keep them happy. During busy times, keep idle chatter to a minimum. Keep mistakes in ordering food to a minimum. Communicate any special cooking requests clearly and articulately. Pick up your food promptly. Repeat: *Pick up your food promptly.*

Some restaurants have either an expediter or a food runner, or both. The *expediter* works opposite the chefs, combining plates to complete orders for individual tables and coordinating interaction between the back and front of the house. A *food runner* delivers orders to the wait person or directly to the table.

Chef

Chef is French for "leader" or "chief," and the chef is definitely in charge of all the kitchen activities. The chef's most important job is the selection and planning of the menu. Restaurant chefs are either trained at culinary schools or learn their skills on the job, moving up to work with better and better chefs. This is usually the highest-paid position in the restaurant, and for good reason. The chef is responsible for the food, and the food is the reason for the business. Discriminating taste and physical stamina are important traits for any chef. A larger restaurant may also have a *chef de cuisine,* or executive chef, who establishes the menu and style of the cuisine. In addition, a larger restaurant may employ a pastry chef, who is in charge of all desserts, and a baker.

Sous-Chef

A larger restaurant may also have a *sous-chef.* This term is French for "under chef." The sous-chef is the number-one backup person for the chef. He or she cooks alongside the chef or in place of the chef. When the chef is not around, the sous-chef is in charge of the kitchen staff. The chef (or chef de cuisine) sets the style of cooking; the sous-chef follows this style. Sous-chefs share and assist the chef in administrative duties. They also do actual cooking and supervise the other cooks.

Line Cooks

The section of the kitchen where the grill, stoves, fryers, and pantry are located is called *the line.* The people who work here are called *line cooks.* Some line cooks are specialized. One may be the grill cook; another may be the sauté cook. The chef sometimes "works the line" to speed things up.

The section of the line where the cold foods are prepared is called the *pantry,* or *cold station.* These foods include cold appetizers, salads, and desserts. The cooks who work there are called *pantry cooks,* or *garde mangers* [guard mon-JAY], another French term.

Burns are an occupational hazard for line cooks. Be sympathetic when you see one of your teammates with a bandage. He or she might have been injured while helping you make money.

Prep Cooks

Kitchen employees who prepare the food to be cooked are called *prep cooks.* Prep cooks chop vegetables, make salads and salad dressings, thaw foods, and so on. They do all of the preparation of the food before the cooks actually cook it. Knife wounds are an occupational hazard for prep cooks. Again, be sympathetic.

Dishwashers

Dishwashers are critical members of the house team. They load plates, glasses, and silverware into the dishwashing machines and scrub pots and pans by hand. They make sure the dishwashing machines are working properly, and they usually take out all of the kitchen trash.

Dishwashers are usually the most under-respected and lowest-paid kitchen employees. But without the dishwasher, you would not be able to deliver good service. The best way to show your respect for their efforts is to follow the restaurant procedures for the dish area carefully. Sort silverware properly. Load glass racks correctly. Don't send trash into the dish area for the dishwashers to dispose of. And, of course, thank the dishwashers when they do a good job.

Never, ever discuss your tips with or in front of the kitchen staff. If a back-of-the-house employee helps you out of a bad situation—say you forget to turn an order in and he or she rushes the food out for you—it's a good idea to thank that person with some cash. Consider it an investment.

As we said earlier, it's a tough job to understand the house. Each restaurant has slightly different responsibilities for different jobs. The most important thing to remember is that the other people in the restaurant are your teammates. You have to know them and work closely with them to win the waiting game.

ON YOUR OWN

Visit a restaurant and observe the staff. Can you identify their jobs? Who is the host? Is there a sommelier? Does the bartender have a bar back?

CHAPTER 2

SETTING THE SCENE

The waiting game begins long before guests arrive at a restaurant. Setting the proper scene for waiting tables includes both internal and external preparation. Wait persons must prepare themselves mentally to provide service that meets or exceeds their guests' expectations and to demonstrate the kind of hospitality that will attract repeat business. At the same time, the wait staff must prepare their physical appearance and the physical appearance of the restaurant so that guests feel welcome and comfortable. It's all part of what we call "setting the scene."

The Dining Experience

When people dine at a restaurant, they are buying more than food and beverages; they are buying a dining experience. Guest expectations are a big part of that overall experience. Those expectations depend on the reputation of the restaurant, the style of service offered by the restaurant, and the amount of money the guest expects to pay. Your goal as a wait person is to meet and exceed the guest's expectations. When people leave your restaurant, they should feel that their experience was worth the price. If they feel that their dining experience was not worth the price, they will not come back.

Restaurants can control the following three important factors that determine the guest's dining experience:

- Atmosphere
- Food
- Service

The atmosphere of a restaurant is the overall impression that the restaurant creates through its treatment of space, decor, and lighting. Some restaurants strive for a homey atmosphere, with warm lighting and comfortable chairs. Others strive for a more formal atmosphere, with starker decorations and dramatic lighting. The food is created to match the atmosphere: comfort food in a more relaxed restaurant, haute cuisine in a more formal restaurant.

Although restaurants go to great expense to create the proper atmosphere and serve memorable food, the atmosphere and food are usually *not* the most important factors in determining the dining experience of the guest. The most important aspect of the dining experience for guest satisfaction is the *service*.

As a wait person, you only have limited control over the atmosphere and the food of your restaurant. However, you have a great deal of control over the quality of service you provide for each guest. It is your job to ensure each individual the best possible dining experience by providing excellent service.

Remember: The better the service, the better the guest's dining experience—and the better the guest's dining experience, the better the tip.

If you know what you like and don't like wait staff to do, you have a good basic understanding of the elements of good service. As you can probably guess, the first thing a wait person has to demonstrate to guests is hospitality.

ON YOUR OWN

To make sure your guests have a great dining experience, you must remember what it is like to be a guest. Go out to eat at a full-service restaurant. After dinner, fill in the blanks.

I hate it when my waiter:

_____

_____

_____

I love it when my waiter:

_____

_____

_____

Hospitality

Hospitality is the art of making your guests feel welcome in your restaurant, just as you make guests welcome in your own home. Hospitality is important because:

- It lets your guests know you care.
- It gives your guests confidence in your abilities.
- It helps your guests relax.

You demonstrate hospitality by doing the following:

1. Make a great first impression.
2. Greet your guests promptly.
3. Smile and make eye contact with each guest.
4. Be friendly but not familiar.
5. Read the table.

✳ REAL-WORLD EXPERIENCE ✳

 Uh-Oh Service was a little disappointing. Our waiter was never rude, but simply offered routine service and was clearly just an "order taker." Service was not at all personalized. He offered the same level of service to all of the tables in his station.

Cheers Our waiter was very pleasant and courteous. Although he was professional, he was still personable and relaxed. His attitude made us feel comfortable and welcome.

Good manners demonstrate consideration for others. You expect your guests to be considerate toward you, and likewise, your guests expect you to exhibit good manners toward them. The easiest way for you to do this is by maintaining a welcoming attitude. Smile and make eye contact with your guests. Give them your full attention when you are at their table. Be yourself. Let your own personality come through. And have some fun.

Above all else, your guests should feel a genuine sense of welcome from you. This is in your best interest. Every guest who feels comfortable with you becomes part of your clientele, meaning people who request to be served by you. When guests request you, everyone wins: you, the guest, and the restaurant.

Make a Great First Impression

First impressions are absolutely crucial in the restaurant business. The impression you make on guests in the first thirty seconds of contact will set the tone for their dining experience and may even determine the amount of your tip.

In many restaurants, the host is the first person to greet the guests. The host is responsible for seating guests and making sure they feel welcome. The first impression the host makes is important, but it is not as important as the first impression made by the wait staff since the wait staff has much more responsibility for guests' overall dining experience than the host. Of course, if you happen to work as a host, do your best to make an excellent first impression.

18

GOOD GROOMING

Nothing makes a better impression than good grooming. A well-groomed appearance communicates credibility and professionalism.

Your uniform should be cleaned and pressed. Make sure your hands and fingernails are clean and your hair is properly groomed. Always present a professional image to your guests. Bring to work the tools you need to do your job—pens, a wine tool, and so on—if they are not supplied to you at the restaurant.

Hair: clean and professionally cut

Shirt: pressed and spotless

Apron (or other uniform): pressed and spotless

Nails: clean, trimmed, and well-kept

Pants: well fitting and not faded

Shoes: polished

✳ REAL-WORLD EXPERIENCE ✳

 Uh-Oh Although our waitress was very nice, we were concerned about what sort of service we were going to receive from her because of our first impression. Her shirt was wrinkled and her apron was dirty.

Cheers When our waitress approached our table, we immediately noticed she was well groomed and had a professional appearance.

If you look sharp, guests will assume that you are sharp, that you take pride in your work, and that you will deliver great service.

SIDE WORK

Achieving a good first impression also requires that the restaurant itself make a good first impression on guests. You do your part in this by maintaining your section of the restaurant. Your *section* is the part of the restaurant in which the tables you serve are located.

Your section is your main area of responsibility. Just as you must make sure that you are clean and well groomed, you must also make sure that your section is clean and well groomed. The preparation of your section and the other tasks that you must do before the arrival of guests are referred to as *side work.*

Different restaurants require different kinds of side work. Each restaurant has its own side work for each section. Common side work for a section includes:

- Filling and cleaning salt and pepper shakers and sugar caddies
- Cleaning chairs of any food or debris

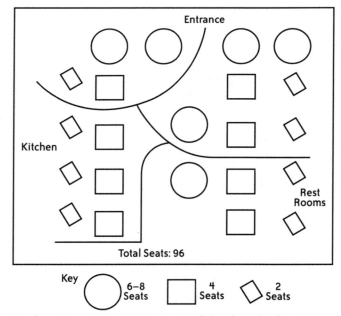

Each restaurant has its own way of dividing the floor into sections, as shown here.

20

- Arranging tablecloths and napkins
- Putting the proper cover, or setting, on the tables

Whatever side work your restaurant requires, do it and do it well. Having a well-maintained section will make all the difference when you're *in the weeds* (that is, when you are so busy it is difficult to deliver proper service). Members of a wait staff must work together to please the guests in all sections at all times. Adopt a team attitude. If you see coworkers in the weeds, help them out.

ON POINT

Also crucial to creating a great impression is making sure everything in your section is *on point*, meaning that everything is properly aligned. The tables should be properly aligned to each other and the dining room. The silverware, condiments, table tents (that is, small announcements of special information, such as drink specials, usually held in an upright stand), and everything else on the tables should be properly aligned with each other.

Sit down at a table and check your section from the guests' eye level for cleanliness and preparation. Make sure that all the tables are level and stable. Learn how to level the tables in your section.

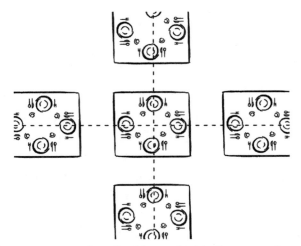

On point means that all tables and table items are aligned.

21

Chairs should also be on point, evenly placed around the table and not pushed all the way under the table. The chairs must also be clean of any food or debris. If the table has a candle on it, light it before the guests arrive or after they arrive if that is your restaurant's policy. Take great care to ensure that everything is ready for your first guests.

TABLECLOTHS AND NAPKINS

Restaurants use cloth tablecloths and placed napkins to create a formal appearance. Each restaurant has its own rules for arranging tablecloths on the tables. Follow those rules and always make sure that the tablecloths you use are clean and not wrinkled. Tablecloths should have a crisp finish to them.

Cloth napkins are standard in most American-service restaurants. Always fold napkins according to the rules of the restaurant, and remember that cloth napkins are very expensive to maintain. Never use napkins or tablecloths to clean spills. Use service napkins for handling hot plates and for serving wine and champagne.

TABLE SETTING

Each restaurant has its own standards for how the table is to be set, depending on the atmosphere the restaurant is trying to create. A *roll-up* (silverware rolled into a napkin) is an informal table setting. A very formal place setting has every piece of silverware needed for a five-course meal.

While there is some variation between restaurants, most restaurants observe these rules for a proper table setting:

- All utensils, plates, and glasses should be spotlessly clean.
- Place forks on the left side of the setting. If there is a salad fork, place it to the left of the dinner fork.
- Place knives to the right side of the setting, and make sure that knife blades face inward. If there is a butter knife, place it to the left of the dinner knife or on the butter plate.
- Place the spoons to the right of the knife: dessert spoon, teaspoon, then soupspoon.

- All utensils are placed about 1 inch from the edge of the table.
- Place the bread plate to the left of the forks, about 1 inch away.
- Place the water glass directly above the dinner knife.
- Place the wineglass to the right and down from the water glass, directly above the teaspoon.

A typical table setting

ON YOUR OWN

Take out a sheet of paper and draw a proper table setting. Remember that each restaurant has a slightly different table setting. It may seem confusing at first, but setting the table according to the standards of your restaurant will soon become second nature to you.

Greet Your Guests Promptly

It is important to greet your guests promptly; this is a critical time for establishing a good server-guest relationship. Guests want to know who their server is. They also want to be sure that their server is going to pay attention to them. If your restaurant does not have a time standard for greeting guests, set one for yourself: greet your guests within two minutes after they have been seated.

✳ REAL-WORLD EXPERIENCE ✳

 Uh-Oh A full five minutes went by and no one spoke to us. Finally, a waitress approached us and cheerfully offered something to drink, but never apologized or gave an explanation as to why we were ignored for so long.

 Cheers The restaurant was very busy. We hadn't been seated long when a young woman appeared at our table. She introduced herself as our waitress and told us she would be right back to take our drink order.

Do you like to feel ignored? Of course you don't. And neither do your guests. Try to greet your guests within two minutes after they have been seated. If you take longer than two minutes, the guests may begin to wonder if you know they exist. If you cannot get to your table to greet them promptly, at least approach your guests, identify yourself, and tell them you will be right back. That way, they won't feel ignored.

"I like to see how many of the guests' names I can remember in one night. I get the names from the reservation list, and make a game out of how many I can remember."

Smile and Make Eye Contact with Each Guest

Nothing makes a guest feel more comfortable than a smile. Take a few seconds with each person to make eye contact and smile. This is good manners—and shows genuine warmth. Also, take this opportunity to determine who is the host of the table, if there is one. The host is the person who is "in charge" of the table, and who will take responsibility for paying the bill and ordering certain items such as wine. Often, the host is the first to talk to the wait person, or to ask the wait person to take orders or give the table more time to make decisions.

Continue to make eye contact with your guests throughout their meal, particularly with the person hosting the table, if you can identify one; he or she may discreetly signal you to clear the table, pour more wine, or bring the check. Eye contact will demonstrate your continuing hospitality and will help make sure that you give your guests your full attention whenever you are at their table. The guests should be the center of attention in any restaurant and the center of your attention when you are at their table.

Be Friendly but Not Familiar

Guests want to experience a flow of communication with the wait staff. The best service is always circular: the diners and the wait person exchange information. Initiate a positive experience for them by providing a warm greeting. Be professional, courteous, and friendly, but not overly familiar. If you address a guest by name, use only their correct title and last name, never their first name. Smile and say something like: "Good evening, Mr. Jones. Welcome to (name of your restaurant)."

✳ REAL-WORLD EXPERIENCE ✳

Uh-Oh Although she started off on a pleasant note, our server became more and more intrusive during our meal. As she placed the dishes in front of us, she was constantly making comments. When we left the restaurant, we felt like she had dined with us.

Cheers Our server was very professional. She quietly and efficiently went about her duties. She was available but did not hover over our table. She was respectful of our conversation. When she did need to speak with us, she timed herself so she did not interrupt the flow of our business meeting.

Polite, friendly service does not mean being loud and overly familiar with your guests. Remember that you are building a business relationship, and guests expect to be treated in a warm but businesslike manner.

Read the Table

When you begin conversing with your guests, you should read the table quickly and accurately to determine what kind of service your guests want and need. Reading a table is like being a detective. You must pick up on clues to figure out who your guests are and what kind of hospitality they want. What kind of clothes are they wearing? Golf clothes? Tuxedos? Business suits? Do they seem to be businesspeople, tourists, couples, or some other kind of guest? Are they nervous or relaxed? Is there one person hosting the table?

After you have made an educated guess as to who your guests are, you will have a better idea of what kind of service they want. People conducting a business lunch or dinner usually want formal and businesslike service, as unobtrusive as possible. The host of the table may have made some of the arrangements with the restaurant in advance to insure minimal interruptions. Tourists might appreciate informal and chatty service. And couples usually want the wait person to be invisible.

Remember: While you are reading the table, the guests are reading you as well. Be polite and proper, and show them real, honest-to-goodness hospitality.

Demonstrate hospitality, read your table, and deliver the kind of service that each different guest wants. But no matter whom you are serving, make them feel welcome throughout the meal. Let your personality shine through and have fun!

ON YOUR OWN

Go out to a restaurant with a friend and look around at the different guests. How many different kinds of guests can you identify? Make a list. Next to each different kind of guest, write down the type of service that would be most appropriate. As new guests come into the restaurant, see how quickly you can read them and determine the type of service they would enjoy most.

CHAPTER 3

OWNING THE MENU

Recommending and describing food is an important part of your job. As a wait person, you need to be more than just an order taker. Guests are at your restaurant to have a good meal and often want or need help with their decisions. Sometimes they might not be familiar with foods listed on the menu, or they might be over-whelmed by a wide variety of menu choices.  To be helpful, you must be knowledgeable about everything the restaurant offers. You must be ready to explain any dishes on the menu and help people narrow down their options and make menu selections that they will thoroughly enjoy.

Use the proper vocabulary to describe the different menu items. *Fresh, caramelized, homemade, crisp, light, creamy, spicy,* or other descriptive words help the diner form a mental picture of a dish. (See pages 134 to 139 for a glossary of descriptive terms.) Be ready with an honest answer to the questions, "What do you recommend?" or "What's good tonight?" Sincerely recommend your favorites. And if guests ask for your opinion, don't be afraid to steer them away from dishes that you personally do not like.

Encourage guests to ask questions so they can make informed decisions about what they want to order. Be ready with answers to questions such as:

- What is in the potato and leek soup?
- How spicy is the blackened redfish?
- Can I get the sauce on the side?
- Is the pasta dish a vegetarian item?

You need to know what ingredients are in each dish. Don't try to bluff; you'll lose customer confidence.

The best way to learn the menu is to take it home with you and memorize it. Sit down with another wait person and quiz each other on the different dishes on the menu. If you are not sure about the ingredients in a particular dish, ask a member of the kitchen staff. If your restaurant features daily or seasonal specials, make sure you know their ingredients, as well as how they are prepared. You should always attend menu tastings of dishes so that you will be able to speak from experience when describing a menu item.

ON YOUR OWN

Visit several full-service restaurants and ask if you can have a copy of their menu. Restaurant websites usually have menus posted. *Gourmet*, *Bon Appétit*, and *Food & Wine* magazines list seasonal menus with the latest popular ingredients. Practice describing dishes from these menus with a few friends. See who can describe a dish in the most appealing way.

Many restaurants have a menu that changes daily or seasonally, depending on the food items that are available at certain times of the year. Pay close attention at staff meetings where menu changes are discussed. If you have any questions about the ingredients in a menu item, be sure to ask. And always taste new menu items when possible. It is often easier to recall the ingredients of a menu item if you can also recall the taste.

Dietary Restrictions

It is important that you know the ingredients of each dish on the menu because diners who suffer from food allergies must be very particular about the foods they eat. Others may not be allergic to certain foods, but may observe dietary restrictions for religious, personal, or health reasons.

Food allergies are a serious issue and must be treated with great concern. Some allergies are so serious that a person can die if he or she eats nuts, wheat, shellfish, or another food. When a guest asks if a certain dish contains a particular food, do not guess. Some menu items may contain ingredients that will surprise you. Caesar salads, for example, may contain raw eggs. If you do not know the answer, ask the chef or manager. People have ended up sick or even dead because a wait person guessed about the ingredients in a dish.

According to an article by F. Speer, published in *American Family Physician*, people are most commonly allergic to the following ten foods: cow's milk, chocolate and cola, corn, eggs, peanuts and other foods of the pea family, citrus fruit, tomatoes, wheat and other grains, cinnamon, and artificial food colorings. If a guest has an allergic reaction, call 911 immediately.

"Once a customer asked me if the apple pie had nuts in it and instead of checking with the kitchen, I said no. Well, the crumb topping had pecans in it; the customer ended up in the hospital, and I ended up being fired."

Some guests may ask about the ingredients in a dish because they follow certain religious or health rules concerning the foods they eat. Some dietary restrictions include:

Kosher: Some Jews restrict their diet to foods that are kosher, meaning permissible for consumption according to Jewish dietary laws. These require that animals be raised on organic food and killed humanely. Some Jews are stricter in their observance of dietary laws than others, but many Jews do not eat pork or shellfish.

Halal: Many Muslims restrict their diets to foods that are halal, meaning permissible for consumption according to Islamic dietary laws. Most Muslims do not eat pork or drink alcoholic beverages.

Vegetarianism: Vegetarians avoid eating meat, but vegetarians are of varying strictness. *Ovo-lacto* vegetarians do not eat any meat but do allow animal products, such as milk, eggs, butter, cheese, and honey. Vegetarians following a *vegan* diet avoid all meat and animal products. Be familiar with the vegetarian options on the menu. Be aware that some dishes may be cooked with meat stock even though they appear to be vegetarian.

Lactose-intolerance: People who are lactose intolerant must avoid foods that have milk, cream, or other milk products.

Low-fat dieting: Many people avoid fatty foods such as cream or butter, either to lose weight or because of health concerns. Some people specifically avoid saturated fats, found in animal products and coconut milk, while others specifically avoid hydrogenated fats, found in most margarines and vegetable shortenings.

Low-carb dieting: People who follow some low-carb diets avoid certain kinds of carbohydrates, such as potatoes, white rice, and bread.

✳ REAL-WORLD EXPERIENCE ✳

 Uh-Oh My friend asked if the crab cakes were served with vegetables, and the waiter replied that yes they were, including asparagus. When the dish arrived, it was served atop a generous portion of seasoned rice with no vegetables. We were very disappointed.

 Cheers Our waiter's menu knowledge was impeccable. We loved his descriptions of the specials of the evening. He was pleasant and unhurried, and he seemed genuinely interested in helping us decide what to order.

The waiting game is a sales game, and the product you are selling is food. To sell the food in your restaurant, you have to know the ingredients of all of the menu items and how each dish is prepared. These days, more and more restaurant-goers have dietary concerns or food allergies and may ask specific questions about how food is served and prepared. Food allergies are a serious issue and must be treated with great concern. Knowing as much as possible about the food you serve will make your job easier and safer.

Beverages

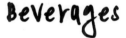

Beverages are as important as food. Offer your guests beverages when you greet them, or when you give them their menus. Prompt, accurate beverage service is important. For many people, a great dining experience begins with great beverage service.

As you take the diners' beverage orders, be sure to tell them about the beverages offered by your restaurant. If the restaurant has a specialty drink or is featuring a new wine by the glass, tell your guests.

Since many people do not consume alcohol, be ready to suggest a variety of nonalcoholic beverages. Some popular ones include mineral water (still and carbonated), flavored iced tea, juice, and nonalcoholic beer and wine.

Liquor

Mention bar specials or popular *cocktails*, drinks made with alcohol. Many people are *brand loyal*, which means that if they order a cocktail, they will ask for a particular brand of liquor to be used in the cocktail—a Tanqueray martini, for example, or an Absolut vodka and tonic. If a guest does not specify a brand, ask if he or she has a preference and mention a brand name. "Would you like any special tequila in your margarita? May I suggest our Herradura Silver margarita?"

Premium liquor costs more but usually tastes better than *well liquor*, or liquor that is not asked for by name. By helping a guest specify a brand of premium liquor, you will increase his or her satisfaction—and the size of the check. (For more on alcoholic beverages, see chapter 6).

Wine

Don't be afraid of wine. It may seem complicated, but it is nothing more than fermented grape juice. You do not have to be a wine expert, but you should keep the following wine essentials in mind:

- Wine complements the food and adds to the guest's dining experience.
- Certain wines go best with certain foods.
- Wine increases the size of the check.

You should also be able to recommend the following wines:

- An inexpensive and an expensive white wine
- An inexpensive and an expensive red wine
- Two wines for each entrée
- An after-dinner wine

Study the wine list in the restaurant and talk with your coworkers about the various wines your restaurant offers. Continue learning about wine by tasting it, keeping a wine notebook, reading about it, and attending all the wine seminars your restaurant offers. (For more on wine, see chapter 7.)

Guiding the Selection

Each restaurant has its own way of describing the menu items for the guests. Many restaurants offer specials of the day, which you are expected to describe. Make sure your description of the special is accurate and appetizing. If there are no specials, ask if the guests have any questions about the menu or need more details about a certain selection.

Take care to find out what kind of food the guests are looking for. If a person hesitates while ordering, help him or her choose a menu item by asking questions such as "Are you looking for a hearty meal or something lighter?" or "Do you like flavorful, spicy dishes or something milder?" The closer a dish matches the guest's desire, the greater his or her satisfaction with the restaurant and with you as a server.

Diners appreciate honest opinions about food. Recommend dishes that you clearly like. Diners also like to feel that they have ordered well. Compliment their selection. "The lamb is excellent." Smile or nod approvingly.

Every day, you must know not only the specials, but also what menu items have been 86ed. If an item is *86ed*, it means that it is unavailable at that time. If the restaurant is out of a popular item, have an alternative ready to suggest to your guests. Be positive about suggesting substitute foods. "The lamb special has been very popular tonight and is no longer available. The chef recommends the beef tenderloin with the béarnaise sauce."

If a guest has a specific question about an ingredient in a dish, make sure you know the answer. Knowing the ingredients of each dish on the menu will make your job easier and safer. (For more on specific foods and ingredients, see chapter 8.)

taking and Placing Orders

When the guests have decided what they want, take their order. Do not rush them. Pick up on clues that show they are ready to order. Are they closing their menus? Are they looking around? If guests have any further questions about the menu, answer them patiently.

When the guests are ready, listen carefully to each order. If someone makes a special request, be sure that you understand what he or she wants. If you are not sure about an order, repeat it back. Always double-check any orders that involve special dietary requests. Pay close attention to the all the orders so that you will be able to relay them accurately to the kitchen.

You must remember which guest ordered what, so that when you serve, you will be able to get the right food to the right person. If there is an extra charge for any special order or request, be sure to inform the guest. Your restaurant may have a system for you to use when writing down the orders. Different systems include using preprinted order checks or using a shorthand system such as chair order to identify guests. *Chair order* is a system in which every chair at a table is given a particular number. Familiarize yourself with the restaurant's ordering system and use it.

The other half of taking the order is placing it. *Placing the order* means communicating the orders clearly and accurately to the kitchen. Each restaurant has its own system for placing orders. Most restaurants use a *point-of-sale (POS) system,* a computerized ordering system that keeps track of each check, sends orders to the kitchen, and generates sales reports at the end of the shift.

No matter what type of order-placing system your restaurant uses, always double-check the order before you send it to the kitchen, and make sure to communicate special orders and dietary requests. The surest way to make a chef angry is to place wrong orders or pick up someone else's order.

Proper timing

If you want to win the waiting game, timing is crucial. Nothing is more annoying to a diner than waiting too long for a meal or being rushed to finish. As a wait person, your job is to allow guests the time they need to enjoy their meal, while allowing the kitchen enough time to prepare the food properly. Different restaurants use different systems to help deliver courses on time.

In most restaurants, you order each course when you need it. This system places the responsibility for timing on you, the wait person. You must be able to estimate how long different courses take to cook and to eat. For example: A guest orders a salad and an entrée. You know that the entrée takes eight minutes to cook and that the guest will take about eight minutes to eat the salad. So you place the order for the entrée right after you serve the salad.

In order to time your courses perfectly, you also need to watch out for the following factors that can slow down cooking times:

- The kitchen is short-staffed.
- There is a banquet or a large table that is slowing the kitchen down.
- The kitchen is working with a new menu.
- The restaurant is extremely busy.
- There are equipment or supply problems.

Keep aware of the situation before and during each shift. Adjust your timing accordingly. As you gain experience, you will develop a mental clock that will help you time your service properly, and proper timing will become second nature to you.

CHAPTER 4

Serving and Clearing Properly

Using proper serving and clearing techniques adds style and professionalism to your performance as a wait person. A knowledge of proper serving and clearing techniques separates a great wait person from an average wait person and changes an average tip into a large tip.

Serving and clearing is a dance that you perform with your guests. You lead the dance, and the guests follow. You must know the steps of the dance, you must be graceful, and you must have a certain rhythm when performing your serving and clearing tasks. Above all else, you have to respect your guests' personal space, and you must follow the rules.

THE TEN RULES OF SERVING

1. Hold silverware, glasses, and plates properly (see illustrations on page 40).
2. Bring everyone's food to the table at the same time.
3. Know what dish goes to which guest.

4. Serve women first.

5. Serve food from the left side of the guest.

6. Serve beverages from the right side of the guest.

7. Place the plate on the table so that the entrée is closest to the guest.

8. Perform table maintenance as needed.

9. Make sure that the guests' food is to their liking.

10. Respect the guests' personal space.

Always hold silverware by the handle, never by the end that will touch the food.

THE FIVE RULES OF CLEARING

1. Wait until everyone has finished eating before you begin clearing.

2. Remove plates and glasses from the right side of the guest.

3. Remove plates from the table one at a time. Never stack dirty plates on the table.

4. Remove plates, glasses, and silverware quickly, quietly, and efficiently.

5. Respect the guests' personal space.

Always hold glasses by the stem, never by the rim.

Always hold plates so that your thumb rests on the outside edge of the plate.

Remember that you always serve plates from the left side of the guest and clear them from the right—or, *lower left, raise right (LL RR)*. Always try to avoid reaching across a guest. If a guest is seated against a wall or in a booth so that you have to reach across someone else to serve him or her, try to do it as quickly and unobtrusively as possible.

Serving and removing plates is what waiting tables is all about. This is no place to get creative. No matter what course you are serving or clearing, follow these rules unless it is intrusive to do so.

✳ REAL-WORLD EXPERIENCE ✳

 Uh-Oh Our waiter stood between my guest and me while we were trying to talk. While he was serving the entrée, he bumped my arm, and I spilled red wine all over the table. If he had served the food from the left, the accident would never have happened.

Cheers Our waiter was graceful and unobtrusive. It was as if things just appeared at our table. We never felt like we were in the way of our waiter serving us.

Proper service techniques are simple and are based on well-established rules. Following these rules adds style and professionalism to your service.

Tray Service

To be a successful wait person, you have to master the balancing act of using trays. As you learn more about waiting tables, you will find that your most important tool is the tray. The tray is an extension of your hand and gives you the following benefits:

- Better serving efficiency
- Better serving style
- Better control over spills and other accidents
- Better sanitation

There are two types of trays that servers use. Large oval trays, called *service* or *hotel trays,* are used for carrying plates to and from the table. Small, usually round trays, called *drink* or *cocktail trays,* are for carrying beverages. Both types of trays come in different sizes.

Regardless of the size or style of the tray, it is extremely important to keep trays clean and sanitary. Never set utensils or food directly on the tray. Always set them on a plate or napkin so that the tray does not get dirty.

It is important to make sure the bottom of the tray is clean and dry. You will not have control of the tray if it is greasy and dirty. *Tray jacks,* also known as *tray stands,* are used to set trays on in the dining room, and they also need to be kept clean.

Service Trays

Carry service trays with whatever hand is most comfortable for you. Always put the tray on a tray jack before serving the food. Serving food from a tray while you are holding it is unsightly and unsafe, because you don't have much control if you're trying to balance the tray and serve food at the same time.

When loading a tray with food dishes, position the plates to evenly balance the load. If possible, the heaviest items should be placed on the side of the tray that will be closest to your body. This allows your body to carry a lot of the weight and gives you more control. Plates should never be stacked on top of one another unless plate covers are used. Plate covers are metal or plastic lids that are sometimes placed on plates to protect the food and help keep it warm.

If you're not using plate covers, the rims of the plates may overlap each other, as long as no sauces or other foods on the plate spill or run together. Some restaurants do not allow waiter staff to carry food and drinks on the same tray. Should the

A properly loaded service tray

drink spill into the food, the food will be ruined, and there is no chance of re-plating the food and saving the dish.

Now that you have your clean service tray properly loaded and the weight evenly distributed, you can pick it up. Use your legs, not your back, to lift. Bend your knees, lower your body, and slide the tray out so that your hand is centered underneath. Check the weight distribution and weight of the tray. If it feels stable, slide it onto your shoulder. Move your hand a little past center away from

Always lift trays with your legs, not your back.

your body, and use your shoulder and hand to carry the tray.

Visualize the tray as an extension of your hand while you learn how to balance and carry it. Some servers balance the tray on their fingertips; others balance it on their open, flat hand. Try both methods to learn which works for you. Pick up your tray jack with your free hand and move into the dining room, alerting your coworkers with a "behind you" or "coming through" if needed.

Once you reach your destination, open the tray jack, bend your knees, and set the tray down. Once the tray is safely on the jack, slide the tray so that it is centered on the tray jack. And remember: To avoid injury, use your legs when lifting and lowering heavy trays; don't bend your back.

When bussing a table onto a tray—that is, loading a tray with dirty dishes in the dining room—do not scrape the plates in front of guests. Quietly stack dishes that are the same size together—all of the

A tray jack

bread plates in one pile, saucers in another, silverware together. This system helps in distributing the weight, and makes unloading the tray easier. The most important thing to remember about loading a tray with dirty dishes in the dining room is that it must be done as safely, neatly, and as quietly as possible. A nice touch is to cover the mess with a napkin before carrying it through the dining room to the dishwashing area.

ON YOUR OWN

Many first-time wait persons are worried about handling a large, heavy tray. The secret to tray handling is practice, practice, practice. Get a serving tray, fill some strong plastic bags with dirt or sand, put the bags on the tray, and practice carrying the tray around the house. You may feel foolish at first, but you'll find that carrying a tray becomes second nature to you

---

Drink Trays

When loading a drink tray, place the heavy drinks in the center of the tray. You will have more control and lessen the chances of spilling a drink. Always carry drink trays with the left hand. Unlike serving food from service trays, it is proper to serve beverages directly from your drink tray to the right of the guests.

Arm Service

Arm service is carrying dishes and glasses without using a tray. Some restaurants require wait staff to use this style of service instead of using trays.

The same basic service rules apply to arm service: Serve food from the left and beverages from the right. You must load the plates onto your arm in the correct order so that you will be able to serve women first.

You should be able to load four plates on your arm; three on the right and one in your left hand. If you are left-handed, you may have to do the opposite.

Pick up a plate with your left hand. Place it between your index finger and thumb on the right hand. The index finger should be fully extended, supporting the bottom of the plate. The thumb should be on the rim of the plate. Hold the plate like this until you are comfortable with the feel.

Next, pick up another plate with your left hand. Place it onto the palm of your right hand, under the plate you are holding on to with your thumb and index finger. The rim of the second plate should touch the bottom of the first plate. Your three fingers should be holding the bottom of the second plate. You are now holding two plates in your right hand.

Turn your right hand slightly toward your body. Pick up the third plate with your left hand. Place the third plate on your right forearm, with the bottom of the plate also setting on the rim of the second plate. You now have three plates in your right hand and arm.

Pick up the fourth plate with your left hand. This is

Arm service

going to be the first one you serve, so it should be a woman's plate (if there are any women at the table). Now you're ready to go serve your guests.

As you unload, serve the plates in the opposite order you loaded them. The plate in your left hand is the first one you serve. The third plate you picked up, the one on your forearm, is the second plate you serve. The second plate you picked up, the one on your palm, is the third you serve, and the first plate, on your fingertips, will be the last.

For beverage arm service, standards vary, but you can usually carry up to three glasses in one hand: Open your hand, palm up. The first glass rests on the part of your palm between your index finger and your thumb. The second glass is set on your other three fingers. The third glass sits on the remaining part of your palm.

You can carry two cups of coffee on saucers in one hand, as you did the two dinner plates. Do not attempt to carry a third cup, as you will have such little control you will slosh the coffee onto the saucer.

If a restaurant does not allow trays for bussing, clear from the right, remove the plates one at a time, and stack them on your arm,

out of the way of the guests. Be careful to always remove silverware by the handles and be especially careful not to drop silverware
when clearing dishes. When clearing glassware from a table, always
handle the glasses by the base.

---

*"I wanted to move from hostessing to waiting, but I was afraid of carrying
heavy trays. I wish I'd done it; I should have practiced at home with a large,
loaded tray."*

Serving in Courses

Most restaurants serve the courses of a meal in the following order:

1. Appetizers
2. Soup
3. Salad
4. Entrées

Some restaurants offer entrées *à la carte*, or served as individual
dishes. Other restaurants offer entrées as part of a multicourse dinner.
Tapas and other "small plates" are becoming increasingly popular.
Once you understand the basic rules of serving and clearing, you must
learn how to serve and clear each individual course properly.

Appetizers

If each person at the table has ordered an *appetizer*, a first course
eaten before the main course, serve the appetizer from each guest's
left, and place an appetizer fork to the left of the salad fork.

If the guests are sharing appetizers, place a small plate in front
of each guest from the left, and place the appetizer fork to the left
of the salad fork. Then place the appetizers in the center of the table

for the guests to share. Bring appropriate silverware, such as a serving spoon and forks, for the guests to serve themselves the appetizers. If you really want to impress the guests, serve each person a small portion of each appetizer.

After everyone has finished the appetizer course, remove the used plates and silverware. Clear from the right. Do not stack dirty dishes on the table or in front of the guests.

Crumb the table if necessary. A *crumber* is a folded metal device that is used to clear bread crumbs and food debris from the table. Crumbers work best on tablecloths. To use a crumber, sweep the debris into a small pile, then scoop up the debris. Place the crumbs in your hand, on a tray, or on a small plate. Some restaurants use a crumber that resembles a small dustpan and a little broom. In this case, sweep the debris into the dustpan and remove from the table.

A broom crumber

A metal crumber

Soup

A cup of soup should be served on a saucer, perhaps with a doily between the saucer and the soup cup so the cup does not slide off. A bowl of soup is usually placed on an *underliner,* a larger plate used to help serve. Doilies are often placed on the underliner also. Make sure the sides of the cup or bowl are clean. Wipe off the edge of the cup or bowl if necessary. Serve the cup or bowl of soup from the guest's left, and place the soup spoon to the right of the cup or bowl. If you preset the soup spoon, place it to the right of the knife.

Salad

Serve salads from the left. Most restaurants offer freshly ground pepper from a pepper mill; you grind the pepper from the mill onto the guest's salad. Stand to the left of the guest and offer the guest fresh pepper. Usually, four or five grinds are enough for most people. You may ask if they would like more pepper, but do not tell the guest to "say when." You can adjust the grind on a pepper mill by tightening or loosening the small metal knob on the top of the pepper mill.

Occasionally, guests will need to cut their salad greens with a knife. If they do use their knife with their salad course, you should clear the used knife and bring a clean knife for the next course. If a guest uses the dinner fork to eat the salad, bring a fresh dinner fork.

Remember: Never draw attention to the fact that a guest has used the wrong utensil. Replace used silverware quickly and discreetly after each course.

Grind fresh pepper with a mill.

While clearing the salad course and freshening the table, check for any other items the guests may need with their entrée course.

- Do they need more bread and butter?
- Do they need steak knives?
- Do they need more wine or drinks to complement their entrées?

This is a great time to recommend wine. If the table is drinking wine by the bottle, fill the glasses and suggest another bottle. People are more likely to order a second bottle of wine before the entrées arrive than they are after the entrées are served. Help enrich their dining experience and suggest a wine that will complement their entrée.

Entrées

Serve entrées from the left.

Usually, entrée plates are heated. If the plate is hot, use a *side towel* when handling the plate, and be sure to tell the guests, "Your plate is hot." A side towel is a folded napkin used as a serving tool.

Place steak knives to the right of the entrée plate and to the left of the dinner knife if preset. It is also acceptable to place the knife (blade in) on the upper right rim of the entrée plate in what is called the *two o'clock position*. Do not shove the steak knife under the steak, unless that is customary in your restaurant.

Serve entrées from the left, and always serve women first. Serve the entrée plate so that the main part of the entrée is closest to the guest. In many restaurants wait persons are expected to sprinkle or grate cheese onto certain dishes. Follow your restaurant's procedure, but always be sure to offer the cheese politely, stand to the left of the guest, and sprinkle or grate the cheese as unobtrusively as possible.

Serve the entrée so that the main part is closest to the guest.

After serving the entrées (and filling the wineglasses), ask if there is anything else you may bring for the guests.

During the Meal

It is important that you check back to make sure that everyone is enjoying the meal. The usual standard is two minutes. This is sufficient time for everyone to taste the food. Ask your guests in a positive way if the food is properly prepared. Say something like, "Are you enjoying your dinner?" or "Is there anything else I can get for you?" Try to avoid words like "okay" or "all right."

Maintain the guests' water and beverages throughout the meal. Keep water glasses full but do not refill them after every sip. Water glasses should not get below one-third full.

Remove glasses and coffee cups from the table before refilling them. Pick up glasses from the bottom half of the glass, and pick up coffee cups from the saucer to prevent any accidental spills. Fill them while holding them in the air. Of course, if the restaurant has a different rule about refilling beverages, follow the rule.

If you feel that your presence is needed for something beyond filling the beverage glasses such as serving more bread or taking an order for a beverage, approach the table, stand next to the host, and allow the guests to acknowledge your presence. If this does not work, listen for a break in the conversation and politely interrupt.

During the meal, try to keep your conversation with your guests brief, informative, and pleasant. Talk naturally, but be extremely polite. And avoid the following unappetizing phrases:

- Wrong: "Are you still working on that?"
- Right: "May I remove your plate?"
- Wrong: "What can I get you?"
- Right: "Will you be needing anything else at this time?"
- Wrong: "No problem!"
- Right: "Certainly!"

If you have any doubts about what a guest wants or needs, just ask yourself, "What would I want or need in this situation?" If you are still not sure, politely ask the guest.

Table Maintenance

Table maintenance is one of the things that separates great service from adequate service. Table maintenance means keeping a table neat at all times. In other words, whatever the guest no longer needs disappears from the table. To maintain a table, you must discreetly remove used plates, silverware, and debris as necessary throughout the meal.

Bad table maintenance   Good table maintenance

As you clear each course, maintain the table and prepare for the next course. Clear any food debris by crumbing. Remove glassware that is no longer needed—empty wine or cocktail glasses, for example. Remove the wine bucket when the bottle of wine has been drunk. Remove bread baskets, bread plates, and butter when the entrée course is cleared. A properly maintained table has no empty sugar packets, straws, soiled cocktail napkins, or any other trash on it. Anything that is unsightly or unnecessary is removed from the guests' view.

After you clear a table, mark it with the proper silverware. *Marking a table* means placing the correct silverware on the table before a course is served. The best time to mark a table for the next course is right after clearing the previous course. When marking a table, it is best to carry the new silverware to the table on a silver serving tray or a nice plate. Placing the silverware on a folded linen napkin on top of the carrying tray improves the appearance and sanitation of the presentation.

Table maintenance is more difficult when diners are eating lobster, crab, ribs, corn on the cob, or some other messy food. Restaurants usually offer guests who eat messy foods a way to clean their hands. Some restaurants use a *finger bowl,* a small bowl partially filled with water. Serve the finger bowl on an underliner with a dry napkin and a lemon wedge. The guest squeezes the lemon wedge into the water or onto the fingers to eliminate odors, then uses the napkin to dry his or her hands.

Some restaurants serve guests a warm napkin to clean their hands. To serve a warm napkin, lightly wet a cloth napkin with warm water and place it on an underliner with a lemon wedge. You can also roll the napkin and hand it to the guest with tongs.

After the guest has used either the napkin or the finger bowl, promptly remove it from the table. If the guests look confused about what to do with the napkin or finger bowl, help them out by telling them something like, "Here is something to refresh your hands."

Keep in mind that guests want:

- Professional, courteous service.
- To feel welcomed and thanked for their patronage.
- To be remembered. People love to be remembered! If you can remember your guests' names, what they drink, or something about their last visit to the restaurant, use this information the next time you wait on them.

And guests need:

- Clean silverware, appropriate for each course.
- Food and beverages brought to them.
- Bread, butter, and water maintained.
- Safe food handling.
- A server ready for any request.

Uh-Oh Our entrées were served and the food looked great. But I didn't have a fork, so no one started eating. Our waitress didn't come back to check on us, and by the time I got someone's attention to bring me a fork, everyone's food was cold.

Cheers We told our waitress that we had a plane to catch and were in a bit of a hurry. She helped us choose entrées that were quick to prepare. She even timed everything so that we had enough time to enjoy dessert.

You don't have to be a mind reader to satisfy your guests' wants and needs. Observation, thoughtfulness, and experience will help you provide them with a great dining experience.

Clearing the Table

Wait until all guests have finished their entrées before you clear the table, unless your restaurant has a different rule. If tables are cleared by a *bus person,* or *busser* (a person whose job is just to clean tables), make sure that they start clearing the table at the proper time and finish the job promptly.

Clear a plate before everyone has finished eating only if:

- The guest pushes the plate away.
- The guest starts stacking plates.
- The guest asks you to remove a dirty plate.

If a guest has left a great deal of food on the plate, ask the guest if there is anything wrong with the order. If the guest says there is something wrong, listen to the complaint and offer to remedy the situation by bringing a replacement dish or offering another item from the menu (see chapter 5 for more on handling complaints). If the guest has no complaint, ask if he or she would like the leftovers boxed up to be taken home. After the entrée course is finished, the table should be clear except for teaspoons that may be used for dessert and coffee, and glasses with beverages that are still being consumed. And remember to follow the five clearing rules (see page 40).

Dessert

Dessert is the big payoff at the end of a good meal. Guests often go to a restaurant specifically to enjoy dessert. You can significantly improve the experience of your guests (and increase the check) with dessert sales.

Timing is important in making dessert sales. If you wait too long after the guests have finished their entrées, they may begin to feel full. If this happens, chances are slim that you will make that dessert sale. If people seem disinclined to order dessert, a good technique is to have at least one dessert in mind that is large enough for two people to share. Mention this somewhere in your description. "We have a fresh Key lime pie tonight. Would you like me to bring out a piece with two forks?"

Printed dessert menus and dessert trays that display the dessert offerings are two tools restaurants use to help guests select desserts. In addition to desserts, some restaurants offer a selection of cheeses as an after-dinner course.

✳ TIMING FOR DESSERTS ✳

Desserts have become so important that many restaurants have special pastry chefs to prepare the dessert items. Many of these pastry chefs use elaborate plate presentations with their desserts that can take a long time to create. Be aware of timing issues when requesting such time-consuming dessert preparations from a pastry chef.

After-Dinner Drinks

In addition to offering desserts, always assume that your guests will have after-dinner drinks. Some people will choose to have an after-dinner drink instead of dessert. Make sure that you know what after-dinner drinks and liqueurs the restaurant offers. Mentioning these items is an excellent way to boost your sales.

Coffee is a popular after-dinner drink.

Some guests want coffee either with their dessert, in place of dessert, or after dessert. If the restaurant serves special coffees, be sure to mention them. Some of the most popular are espresso, cappuccino, and caffè latte.

Americano: Espresso diluted with water.
Café au lait: The French version of milk and coffee, which consists of equal parts strong coffee and hot milk.
Caffè latte: Espresso mixed with a large amount of steamed milk and a little foamed milk.
Cappuccino: Espresso mixed with a little steamed milk and topped with foamed milk.
Espresso: Coffee brewed by forcing hot water through finely ground coffee. A cup of espresso measures less than 2 ounces. Sometimes it is served with a lemon peel. The lemon peel is placed on the saucer for guests to twist into the espresso to remove the bitterness.
Mocha: Coffee and hot chocolate.

Some guests prefer tea to coffee, and many restaurants offer an extensive selection of teas. All tea is made from the leaves of a variety of bush. There are more than three thousand kinds of tea, which vary depending on the place of origin, the soil, and the quality and type of the tea leaves. The main types of teas are green, black, oolong, and herbal teas. The difference between green, black, and oolong teas lies in the processing of the tea leaves.

Green teas: Often called "unfermented" teas. Green tea leaves are picked, steamed, and dried to stop the fermentation of the leaves. Some of the most popular green teas are gunpowder, sencha, and silver needle.

Black teas: Teas produced by a complex process in which the leaves are rolled, fermented, and dried. Some popular black teas are lapsang souchong, Darjeeling, and English breakfast.

Oolong teas: Teas made from semi-fermented tea leaves. Oolong (which means "black dragon" in Chinese) teas include peony, white blossom, and monkey-picked.

Herbal teas: Also known as tisanes, these are not actually teas at all, but beverages made from steeping herbs in hot water. The most popular herbal teas include peppermint, chamomile, and lemon verbena.

Teas are served in individual tea bags or in teapots. Tea bags are presented to the table in a tea caddy. Some restaurants use tea strainers or tea balls to steep loose tea and other restaurants use tea caddies, so be sure to know the tea-brewing system used by your restaurant and familiarize yourself with it as quickly as possible.

No matter what type of coffee or tea you are serving, serve the cup on a saucer with the handle pointed at four o'clock. If you can determine that the guest is left-handed, serve the cup with the handle pointed at eight o'clock.

Offer your guests coffee refills. Keep water glasses and tea cups full. Take care of your guests and maintain their tables for as long as they are in your section.

CHAPTER 5

COMPLETING THE DINING EXPERIENCE

If you think that your job as a wait person is over once you have served and cleared the meal, you're wrong. It's just as important to make a great last impression on your guests as it is to make a great first impression, which includes be responsive to all guest requests and complaints during and following the meal, and presenting and processing the check in a swift and professional fashion, and bringing closure to the guests' dining experience.

Handling Complaints

There is an old saying that the customer is always right. In the restaurant business, we know that customers may not always be right, but we still have to make them think they are. To do this, we have to respond quickly and attentively to any guest complaints.

Even if you are not able to make every guest happy, it is absolutely essential that you try. If you ignore a complaint, even an unreasonable one, you will anger your guest. An angry guest will say bad things about your restaurant. And bad word-of-mouth can kill a thriving business.

The best way to handle complaints is to keep them from occurring in the first place. Pay attention to what the guests are ordering. If the food is taking longer than usual to deliver, tell your guests. Stay in contact with your table. A wait person who can anticipate problems and turn a disgruntled guest into a satisfied one has usually made a loyal customer. This can be accomplished by demonstrating that you genuinely care about your guests and that you sincerely wish to make them happy.

Here are some guidelines on how to deal with guest complaints:

- Never argue with an angry guest. Just listen attentively.
- Give the person plenty of time to state the complaint fully, then repeat the complaint back so that he or she knows you have been listening.
- Apologize sincerely. If you can handle the complaint yourself, do so promptly. If you need the assistance of your manager, get that assistance promptly.
- Follow the golden rule and treat your guests in the manner that you would expect to be treated in the same situation.
- View complaints as valuable pieces of information that can help make your service better, not as personal attacks.
- Soothe angry guests with complimentary beverages, appetizers, or other food items.

Some guests will never be satisfied, no matter what you do. Although it can be hard to stay calm when someone is upset with you, don't take it personally. Develop skills to stay composed and professional. Remember that you have other tables to serve. If you let an upset guest ruin your composure, you might end up with more upset guests.

Make sure that you know your restaurant's policy regarding complaints, if there is one. And if a guest is being particularly troublesome, let your manager know.

✳ REAL-WORLD EXPERIENCE ✳

Here are some common complaints heard in restaurants and some improper and proper ways of responding.

Uh-Oh
GUEST: "This isn't what I ordered."
WAITER: "Yes, it is. I wrote it down. You ordered the salmon."

Cheers
GUEST: "This isn't what I ordered."
WAITER: "I'm very sorry. Please tell me again what you wanted and I will make sure the kitchen prepares it right away."

Uh-Oh
GUEST: "Why is it taking so long to get our food?"
WAITER: "We are very busy, ma'am. It takes a while to prepare. Please be patient."

Cheers
GUEST: "Why is it taking so long to get our food?"
WAITER: "Yes, sir. It has been a while on your order. I have just checked with the chef, and it will be only a few more minutes for your food."

Uh-Oh
GUEST: "We're not getting enough service from you!"
WAITER: "Can't you see I'm busy and I'm doing the best I can?"

Cheers
GUEST: "We're not getting enough service from you!"
WAITER: "I'm very sorry I haven't been attentive enough. I will give you my full attention. What can I get for you right now?"

the check

After food and beverages have been consumed and cleared away, you still must perform the delicate task of presenting the check and collecting payment for it. Processing the check promptly, accurately, and courteously is the key to winning the waiting game and earning a 20 percent tip.

In most restaurants, the wait staff processes their own checks. In other words, the wait staff receives the cash, check, or credit card, makes the change or runs the credit card through the payment system, and enters the payment in the payment system. Before you present the check, make sure it is accurate and readable. Check all the prices for the various food and beverage items to make sure that they are correct. The few seconds it takes to review the check can save you from having a big headache if the check is not accurate.

It is not surprising that customers often complain about the check-processing procedures in restaurants. The most common complaints are:

- The prices were wrong.
- The wait staff did not pick up the check quickly enough.
- The wait staff did not process the check quickly enough.

Clearly, the check is a delicate area in the waiting game. Customers are understandably nervous about paying the check. After all, they are being asked to pay for a meal and to pay you a tip for your service as well. It is your job to make the check-paying process as simple, painless, and discreet as possible.

Presenting the Check

Don't be shy about the presenting the check. Be up-front and polite and returning change. Remember that your job does not end until your guests have paid their bill and left the restaurant. Until that time, you have to deliver proper service.

A check presenter

Some restaurants require that you present the check only when a guest asks for it. When the guest asks for the check, present it and process the payment.

Most restaurants require the wait staff to present the check after the dessert course. Ask the guests, "Will there be anything else I can get for you?" If they say no, present the check by placing it to the right of the host. If you can't identify the host, then place the check discreetly in the center of the table.

Many restaurants use a *check presenter,* a folder that holds the check. Place the check presenter to the right of the host or on the edge of the table so that you will notice if the presenter has been moved. If it has been moved, usually it means that someone has paid the check.

After the guest has placed a credit card or cash into the check presenter, process the payment promptly and accurately. Act quickly. Once people pay for their meal, they want their receipt and change quickly.

Always assess the needs of your guests. If they ask for their check during dessert instead of after dessert, present it to them promptly.

✳ REAL-WORLD EXPERIENCE ✳

 Uh-Oh We were having a great experience until the check arrived. We had been charged for some things we did not order. Our waiter had to get a manager to correct the check, and the whole process took a very long time. What had been a great evening ended with a negative impression.

Cheers Our waiter presented the check after dessert was finished and he was certain we didn't want or need anything else. He was right back to process it, and we were on our way.

When guests are ready to leave, they are ready to leave. And when they want their check, they really want their check. Make sure checks are accurate and properly totaled, and process payments quickly and accurately. You may have given your guests great service all through the meal, but if you wait too long to process their check, they will be frustrated. And frustrated guests don't leave big tips.

Paying the Check

Most full-service restaurants do not have a cashier. Each wait person is his or her own cashier during the shift. At the end of the shift, the wait person make one payment to the restaurant. Any shortages may come out of your tips, so be careful when you settle your guests' checks. Guests pay their checks in several different ways: cash, credit cards, checks, and gift certificates.

CASH

Making change can be tricky. The easiest way to make change is to count the cents of the amount due up to the whole dollar, and then count the whole dollars back until you have reached the amount that was given to you. For example, if the check is $13.28 and the guest pays with a twenty-dollar bill, count from $13.28 up to $14.00 (72 cents) and then count out six one-dollar bills until you reach $20.00. If you give the guests six dollar bills, they will have the appropriate amount of money to leave you a 20 percent tip. It is important to bring back proper change for a tip. (Instead of bringing a ten-dollar bill, bring back a five-dollar bill and five one-dollar bills.) Wash and sanitize your hands after handling money whenever possible.

CREDIT CARDS

Most restaurants take credit cards. Credit-card charge vouchers must be filled out correctly. Most credit-card machines are computerized. The amount of the charge is entered into the machine, and a charge voucher is produced. Any altering of credit-card charges, either on the voucher or on the processing machine, is illegal. Any mistakes or corrections must be done while the guest is still in the restaurant, and he or she must initial any corrections. The guest receives a copy of the charge voucher, and the house keeps a copy for payment and for its records. And, of course, remember that it is illegal for you or any of your coworkers to use a guest's credit card number for any purpose other than paying the bill.

CHECKS

If your restaurant accepts checks, follow the necessary procedures. Certain information about the guest needs to be on the check. This usually includes a driver's license number, address, and phone number. This information is needed in case the check bounces and the restaurant has to collect the money directly from the guest.

GIFT CERTIFICATES

Gift certificates are becoming increasingly popular. Follow the restaurant's procedures for accepting a gift certificate.

thank you and farewell

Remember that your job continues after the check is paid. You have to continue to refill the coffee cups and water glasses as long as the guests remain in the restaurant. It would be great if there were a nice way to get lingering guests to clear out for the next table, but there isn't. You just have to be patient.

Closure, the end of the dining experience, is the key to repeat business. When the guests are ready to leave, make eye contact with them, thank them for coming, and invite them to return. You may tell them your name so that they can request your service the next time they come in: "My name is _____, and I've enjoyed serving you. I hope to see you again soon." Something along these lines is acceptable. Offer special assistance if needed, such as opening the door, especially for guests with mobility problems.

You can make a great last impression on your guests by performing various simple acts of courtesy for them as they are preparing to leave. For example, you should:

- Pull out chairs and help with coats.
- Make sure your guests leave with everything they brought with them.
- Thank them sincerely and invite them back.

Making a great last impression requires delivering all the elements of proper service—a prompt greeting, accurate order taking, smooth serving and clearing, and fast, accurate check processing. If the guests have had a great experience from start to finish, they will leave with a wonderful last impression. If a guest returns to your restaurant, congratulations. He or she probably liked your service. And if you can remember a guest's name or something about his or her last visit, let that person know about it—with a smile.

✳ REAL-WORLD EXPERIENCE ✳

 Uh-Oh As I was leaving, the waiter thanked me, but it seemed very routine and not sincere. And I would have appreciated help with the door, since I was on crutches.

 Cheers I was just getting in my car when my waiter came running up to me. I had left my briefcase at the table. I appreciated his efforts so much, as I needed the papers in my briefcase for my afternoon meeting. He thanked me again and said he enjoyed serving me. Great customer service!

Thank your guests sincerely and offer any necessary assistance they may need while they are leaving. And if you enjoyed waiting on them in particular, you should let them know.

CHAPTER 6

ALCOHOLIC BEVERAGE SERVICE

Alcoholic beverage service is an essential part of the dining experience. Proper beverage service is a great way to win the confidence of your guests. Serving beverages promptly and courteously makes guests feel comfortable and relaxed. Once they begin enjoying their beverages, diners begin to feel confident that they will enjoy the rest of their meal.

Serving Alcohol

Alcoholic beverages add to the festive atmosphere of a meal and add substantially to the check total as well. While waiting tables, you will usually handle beverage service for your guests. This means that your beverage service must be **TOPS:**

- **T**ake the drink orders accurately.
- **O**rder the drinks promptly.
- **P**ick up the drinks from the bartender promptly.
- **S**erve them correctly.

Servers must be able to deal with guests and bartenders pleasantly and efficiently. You must be familiar with bar terms, the kind of glassware used, the different brands of liquors and liqueurs, and a variety of cocktails and their variations. You also have to know the rules and laws pertaining to alcohol service.

- Don't serve minors.
- Don't serve intoxicated guests.
- Know your beverages.
- Deliver the drinks promptly.
- Serve from the right side of the guest.
- Serve women first.
- Maintain service throughout the meal.

Don't Serve Minors

Even though it is legal in some states for a minor to consume alcohol, never serve a minor. Always serve the person who is of age, and let that person give the drink to the minor only if it is legal. Be sure you know your local regulations regarding alcohol and minors.

Don't Serve Intoxicated Guests

It is illegal to serve alcohol to an intoxicated person. It may be against the law to even have an intoxicated person in a restaurant. It is also unethical to serve an intoxicated person. Guests deserve better treatment than that. Most states have programs that are designed to teach wait persons and bartenders how to identify an intoxicated person.

If a guest consumes more than the restaurant limit (usually three or four drinks), let the manager know. If you need to *cut the guest off* (refuse alcoholic beverage service), let the guest know that you are concerned about his or her safety. If you have an intoxicated or abusive guest, don't try to handle the situation yourself. Get the bartender or manager to help. Offer to get a taxi for the guest, or a cup of coffee, or make some other goodwill gesture. Deal with the situation as tactfully and quietly as possible, so as not to disturb the other guests.

Know Your Beverages

Always offer a beverage after greeting guests. Mention special drinks or wines if they are available. A great wait person is also able to recognize different types of glassware and to know what drinks are served in each type of glass. In addition, wait persons must know which garnishes go with which drinks.

Deliver the Drinks Promptly

As a wait person, you have to be on good terms with the bartender. Nothing makes a bartender more frustrated than a wait person who submits inaccurate orders or does not pick up drinks quickly. Guests can also be very particular about their beverages and may return a drink if it has sat too long and is watery or not cold enough.

Serve from the Right Side of the Guest

Always serve beverages from the right side, with your right hand. If a guest is left-handed, he or she will switch the beverage to the left side.

Serve Women First

It is always proper to serve beverages to women first. If it is a table of women, serve the first person who ordered and then serve clockwise around the table.

Maintain Service Throughout the Meal

Always let guests finish their drink before offering a second one, but be sure to offer a second one. Assume that your guests will have a second cocktail or glass of wine. And be creative in suggesting an after-dinner drink. Tempt guests with the names and descriptions of some of your restaurant's cognacs or coffee drinks.

STANDARD ALCOHOL BEVERAGE GLASSWARE

Rocks   Old-fashioned   Highball   Collins

Pony/   Sour   Champagne   Martini   Wine
Cordial

Shot Glass/   Brandy Snifter   Margarita   Hurricane
Jigger

A Field Guide to Alcoholic Beverages

Here's a very basic primer for alcoholic beverages. In addition, make sure you read chapter 7, All About Wine, carefully so that you'll feel confident discussing this often daunting subject.

Beer

Restaurant-goers have become increasingly sophisticated about beer. Like wine, beer is a fermented alcoholic beverage. Unlike wine, beer is not fermented from grapes, but from sprouted barley, which is called malt. Malt is dried and roasted. The drying and roasting of the malt determines the darkness and sweetness of the beer. The roasted malt is cooked with water, then cooked with hops, the dried flowers of the hops plant. Yeast is added, causing the liquid to ferment.

Beer is sold either on draft or in bottles. *Draught,* or *draft,* beer is stored in a keg and poured directly into a glass from a serving spout at the bar. Bottled beers are served with an empty glass and poured at the table. To pour beer, place the glass on the table and pour the beer into the center of the glass so that it produces a nice foam or head. Lager, ale, stout, porter, and malt liquor are the main types of beer.

LAGER

Lager is a sparkling, effervescent beer of pale to medium color. Its name is derived from the German verb *lager,* which means "to store." Today, most popular beers are lagers. Some well-known lagers include Budweiser, Heineken, and Beck's. The lager category includes bocks, malts, and pilsners.

Bock: A style of lager that originated in Germany. Bocks are traditionally brewed in the fall, at the end of the growing season, when barley and hops are at their peak. They are then "lagered" all winter and enjoyed in the spring at the beginning of the new

71

brewing season. Bocks can be pale (helles) or dark (dunkles). Double (doppel) bocks are extra strong.

Pilsner: A classic Pilsner has a flowery aroma and tastes of hops. It is a golden color with a firm pale head. Originally from Pilsen, in Czechoslovakia.

ALE

Ale is a generic term for English-style beer. It is fuller-bodied, darker, and more bitter than lager. Some well-known ales include Samuel Adams (Scotch ale) and Samuel Smith (India pale ale). There are also many local ales brewed in small batch breweries and brew pubs all over the United States. There are many popular types of ales.

Bitter ale: A distinctive copper-colored draught beer more heavily hopped than mild, full-bodied ales. Bitter ales sometimes have a slightly malty taste and a low carbon dioxide content.

Brown ale: A traditional beer brewed in England, often quite sweet, darker than bitter and pale ales, and generally sold in bottles or cans.

India pale ale (IPA): Originally brewed in the eighteenth and nineteenth centuries to be transported from England to India and strong enough to withstand the three- or four-month sea voyage.

Mild ale: A draught (or tap) beer, often dark brown in color, with a caramel taste and only lightly hopped.

Pale ale: A livelier beer, faintly acidic, with a strong flavor of hops. Pale ales are generally copper colored.

Scotch ale: A full-bodied, rich ale brewed in Scotland.

Trappist ale: Brewed by Trappist monks at one of six Trappist monasteries in Belgium and Holland. Trappist ales are bottled beers that have yeast added to them right before bottling. The still-active yeast causes the beer to ferment again and a natural carbonation to develop in the bottle.

STOUT

Stout is a beer with a strong hops taste. Made with dark-roasted barley, it was originally called porter. Guinness is a well-known stout.

PORTER

Porter is a type of ale that smells of malt and tastes of hops. It is generally strong, dark, and brewed with soft rather than hard water. Michelob Black and Tan is an example of a porter.

MALT LIQUOR

Malt liquor is a bottom-fermented beer with a high alcohol content. Some states require this term to be applied to all beers of more than 5 percent alcohol by volume.

Liquors

Liquors are distilled alcoholic beverages. They have a higher alcohol content than fermented alcoholic beverages like beer or wine. The alcohol content in both distilled and fermented alcoholic beverages is called *proof.* Each degree of proof is 0.5 percent of alcohol by volume. This means that a 90 proof whiskey is 45 percent alcohol by volume.

A *well brand* of liquor is the brand of liquor poured when the guest does not specify a brand; it is so called because it is kept in a "well," or bin, under the bar instead of on display in shelves behind the bar. The guest may specify a *call brand.* These are the more expensive premium brands and are of higher quality. If a guest requests a liquor beverage, suggest a premium brand.

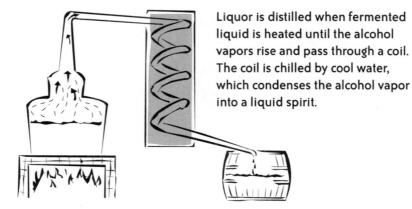

Liquor is distilled when fermented liquid is heated until the alcohol vapors rise and pass through a coil. The coil is chilled by cool water, which condenses the alcohol vapor into a liquid spirit.

Cocktails are mixed drinks made with different types of liquor and one or more other ingredients. Some of the most popular cocktails are martinis, margaritas, Manhattans, gin and tonics, vodka and tonics, bloody Marys, screwdrivers, and daiquiris.

COCKTAIL LIQUORS

TYPE	DESCRIPTION	COCKTAILS	BRANDS
Gin	A neutral spirit flavored with juniper berries and other aromatics	Gin and tonics, martinis, gimlets	Beefeater, Bombay, Bombay Sapphire, Boodles, Cadenhead's Old Raj, Gordon's, Mercury London, Plymouth, Tanqueray, Tanqueray #10
Rum	Distilled from sugarcane	Rum and Cokes, rum punches	Bacardi, Barbancourt, British Royal Navy, Captain Morgan, Castillo, Myers's, Ron Rico
Tequila	Distilled from the fermented juice of the agave plant	Margaritas, tequila sunrises	El Tesoro de Don Felipe Blanco, Herradura, Jose Cuervo, Sauza, Torada
Vodka	Distilled from a fermented mash of grain or potatoes	Vodka martinis, screwdrivers, gimlets, cosmopolitans	Absolut, Fleischmann's, Rain, Smirnoff, Stolichnaya, Taaka

Whiskey is a popular alcoholic beverage distilled from mashed grain and aged in charred oak barrels. Whiskey is usually served as a cocktail, either *on the rocks* (with ice), with water, or *neat* (with nothing added.) A whiskey drinker might want a water or a beer *back* with their whiskey, meaning a glass of water or beer along with their whiskey, served neat or on the rocks.

WHISKEYS

TYPE	DESCRIPTION	BRANDS
Scotch	Distilled in and imported from Scotland, aged at least three years. A single-malt Scotch is a Scotch (spelled whisky) that is made of smoked malted barley and no other grain, and comes from only one distillery, as opposed to a blended Scotch made from barley and other grains.	Single malt: Dalwhinnie, Glenfiddich, The Glenlivet, Oban, Talisker; blended: Cutty Sark, Chivas Regal, Dewar's White Label, J&B, Johnny Walker (Red, Black, Gold, and Blue)
Irish	Distilled in Ireland.	Black Bush, Connemara, Jameson's, Old Bushmills, Tullamore Dew
Canadian	A blend of whiskies made in Canada and aged between three and eight years.	Canadian Club, Canadian Mist, Crown Royal
Bourbon	An unblended whiskey generally made in Kentucky.	Jim Beam, Old Crow, Wild Turkey
Blended	A mixture of straight whiskeys or whiskey and a neutral spirit.	Black Velvet, Hiram Walker, Schenley's
Rye	An American whiskey using a large percentage of rye grain.	Jim Beam Rye, Old Overholt

There are some alcoholic beverages that fall outside the major categories. These beverages may be drunk as cocktails or after-dinner drinks, depending on the tastes and styles of the times. Alcoholic beverages are a lot like clothes—what's in fashion is constantly changing.

OTHER ALCOHOLIC BEVERAGES

TYPE	DESCRIPTION	SERVED AS	BRANDS
Vermouth	A neutral white wine blended with other wines and seasoned with many different herbs and spices. Vermouth is produced in sweet and dry varieties.	A cocktail or after-dinner drink	Martini & Rossi
Cordial	A sweet drink of spirits infused with flavorings; also called a liqueur.	A cocktail or after-dinner drink	Amaretto di Saronno, Anisette, Baileys Irish Cream, Cointreau, Drambuie, Grand Marnier, Kahlúa, Southern Comfort

Sake is a Japanese alcoholic beverage that is made by brewing rice. There are several distinct types of sake, which differ depending on the type of rice used and whether or not alcohol is added to the beverage. Sake is often served warm in small china cups. Popular brands of sake include Juyondai, Kuboto, and Koshi no Kambai.

ON YOUR OWN

Visit a liquor store. Study the different sections that feature the different types of liquor, and become familiar with the different premium brands. Talk with the liquor store owner about customer preferences.

AFTER-DINNER LIQUORS

TYPE	DESCRIPTION	BRANDS
Brandy	A distillation of fermented fruit juices or fruit mash.	Christian Brothers
Cognac	A grape brandy distilled in the Cognac region of France. All Cognac is brandy, but not all brandy is Cognac.	Calvados, Courvoisier VSOP, Rèmy Martin
Port	A sweet dessert wine from Portugal, named for the city of Oporto. Brandy is added to the wine before fermentation.	Croft Tawny Reserve, Fonseca Bin 27
Sherry	A wine fortified with brandy, a product of Spain. Sweet sherries should be served at room temperature; dry sherries are usually served chilled.	Dry Sack, Harvey's Bristol Cream

Nonalcoholic beverages

Some guests may not want to drink alcoholic beverages, but want nonalcoholic ones instead. Nonalcoholic cocktails are sometimes called "mocktails." In some cases, the word *virgin* is used to indicate a cocktail made without alcohol, such as a virgin margarita or a virgin piña colada.

When adults order beverages at a table, be sure to offer the children at the table their own choice of nonalcoholic beverage. Some of the most popular are the "virgin" drinks mentioned above, as well as a Shirley Temple, which is made with Sprite and grenadine and garnished with a cherry; a Roy Rogers, which is made with Coke and grenadine and also garnished with a cherry; or an Arnold Palmer, which is a combination of iced tea and lemonade.

Sparkling water is a popular nonalcoholic beverage for adults. Some sparkling waters come from springs and have a distinctive flavor due to the minerals naturally occurring in the water. Some of the most popular sparkling waters include Pellegrino, Perrier, and Gerolsteiner.

BEVERAGE SERVICE GLOSSARY

Alcohol: Ethyl alcohol, the common ingredient of all liquor.
Aperitif [ah-pair-uh-TEEF]: An aromatic wine usually served before dinner.
Bar back: A person who helps the bartender.
Bitters: Spirits flavored with herbs or fruit; used in cocktails.
Call brand: A brand of liquor poured when the guest asks for a particular brand (as opposed to *well brand*).
Carafe: A pitcher that contains of 1 liter of a beverage.
Free pour: To pour liquor for a drink without using a measure.
Handgun: A dispensing head for an automatic liquor system.
Highball: A mixture of any basic liquor and an additional beverage with ice.
Jigger: A measure for liquor, sized in ounces.
Jockey box: An underbar station unit containing an ice bin and a speed rail, which is the container for the most used liquor bottles, placed in an order for ease of use.
Neat: Alcoholic beverages poured from the bottle into a glass with no ice, water, or other additions.
On the rocks: A drink served with ice.
Proof: A measure of the alcohol content of a spirit, each degree of proof being 0.5 percent alcohol by volume.

Shot: A measure of $1^1/2$ ounces of alcohol.

Straight up: Served without ice.

Twist: A strip of citrus peel used as a garnish for a drink.

Virgin: A cocktail without alcohol.

Well brand: A brand of liquor poured when the guest does not specify a brand (as opposed to *call brand*).

CHAPTER 7

ALL ABOUT WINE

Just as restaurant-goers have become more sophisticated in their food preferences, they have also become more sophisticated about wine. Today, wait persons have to know about wine in order to deliver good service. Guests expect you to know your restaurant's wine list, what wines go with what dishes, and what wines are offered by the glass.

A knowledge of wine and proper wine service is a great way to build customer loyalty and increase revenue. But don't be intimidated or think you have to know everything about wine in order to deliver good service. All you have to do is learn a few basic facts, talk about wine with your coworkers, and sample wines from your restaurant's list. In addition, you may want to keep tasting wines, attend a wine-service training seminar, or visit a winery. Learning about wine is like learning about food. It takes some effort, but it will improve the quality of your service and increase your income.

Wine has become such an important part of the full-service restaurant business that many restaurants now hire a full-time wine specialist, called a *sommelier* [som-el-YAY]. The sommelier is responsible for buying wine, creating the wine list, and answering guests' questions about wines. Working with a sommelier will help you to deliver proper wine service. But even if a restaurant has a sommelier, the servers are expected to answer the following three commonly asked questions about the various wines offered by the restaurant:

- What does it taste like?
- Is it a good value?
- What foods go with it?

What Is Wine?

Wine is nothing more than fermented grape juice. Wine makers grow or buy grapes, crush them, add yeast, and store the juice in a barrel. The yeast ferments the grape juice, turning the sugar in the juice into alcohol and carbon dioxide gas.

If the carbon dioxide gas is allowed to escape, the wine will be *still,* or *flat.* If the gas is trapped, the result is a *sparkling wine* like champagne. A still wine may be stored for months or even years in oak barrels. The wine is then put in a bottle and shipped.

So what's all the mystique about wine? Why are some wines red, some white, some sweet, some dry, some worth a fortune, and some completely worthless? Once again, it all comes down to the grapes. To make a great wine, you need great grapes. Different varieties of grapes have different tastes. But the flavor of individual grapes of the same variety depends on two basic factors: soil and climate. Certain grapes grow best in certain types of soils. Even when they are growing in the perfect soil, grapes must have a long, hot growing season in order to develop great flavor. As the old saying goes, stressed vines, finer wines. If it rains too much, especially towards the end of the growing season, the grapes will absorb water and become relatively tasteless. *Vintage* refers to the year the grapes for a particular wine were grown and picked. When people say that a particular vintage of wine is a good one, they mean that the climate during that year allowed farmers in a particular region to raise flavorful grapes. A bad year is a year in which the grapes were not as flavorful.

HOW WINE IS MADE

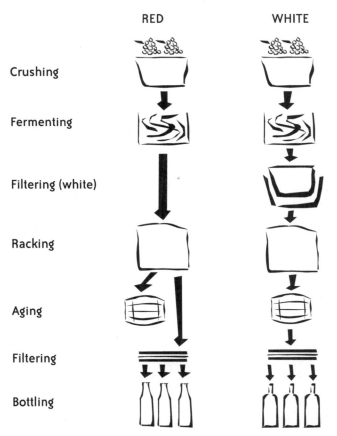

The red color of red wines comes from the grape skins; these are filtered out when making white wine. Though the quality of the grapes is the most important factor in making good wine, wine makers are able to influence how a wine tastes. Wine needs a certain amount of oxygen to age. Too much oxygen can ruin a wine, causing it to lose all color and flavor. Wine makers store wine in oak or steel barrels to add flavor. This is called *aging* the wine. Wine makers have to know how long to age wine before they bottle it. As a general rule, most wines, especially American wines, are ready to drink right after they are bottled.

Wine Basics

Wine itself is pretty easy to understand. What is confusing is the whole culture and vocabulary that has grown up around it. Some of your guests may be wine snobs, who talk endlessly in flowery language about wine. Others may be intimidated by wine. They want to enjoy it, but they don't want to be embarrassed by their lack of knowledge about it. Your job as a wait person is to make your guests feel comfortable. If they know a lot about wine and like to talk about it, let them talk. If they don't know anything about wine, diplomatically help them choose one by suggesting one or two choices from the wine list. Either way, you will have to know how to identify wines and how to talk about them.

There are about fifty thousand different types of wine produced all around the world. California alone produces as many as two thousand different types of wine. You will never taste all of them, so begin by talking with your coworkers about the wines they've tasted. Learn the names and descriptions of a white wine and a red wine to recommend. Learn the name and a brief description of a wine to recommend with each of the entrées. Even if you don't like the taste of a particular wine, learn how to give a neutral description such as "Some people like this wine for its subtlety." Never be negative about a wine. You may be insulting a guest's favorite.

If a guest has very specific questions about the wine list that you cannot answer, find someone to help. If possible, get the manager or wine steward to come to the table and talk about wine with the guest. This will impress the guest, and perhaps increase your tip.

Bottle Size and Label

Most wine comes in 700- or 750-milliliter bottles. Half bottles are one half the size of normal bottles (375 milliliters). Small bottles are called splits, which are half the size of half bottles (187 milliliters). Magnums are larger bottles containing 1.5 liters, twice the size of a normal bottle.

Double magnums, or Jeroboams, contain 3 liters. Bottles get progressively bigger: Rehoboams (4.5 liters), Impériale or Methuselah (6 liters), Salmanazar (9 liters), Balthazar (12 liters), and Nebucadnezzar (30 liters).

The best bottle size for champagne is the magnum, since the champagne ages more gently in a larger bottle. The bottles for champagne and other sparkling wines tend to be thicker than the bottles for still wines, to withstand the pressure within each bottle. A very dry sparkling wine is called *brut* [BROOT].

WINE BOTTLES

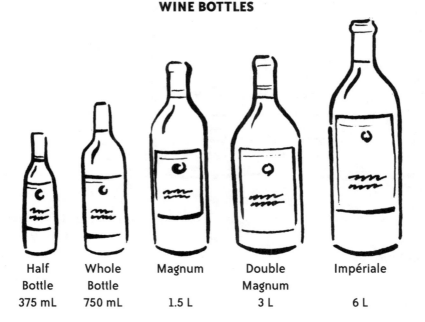

Half Bottle 375 mL	Whole Bottle 750 mL	Magnum 1.5 L	Double Magnum 3 L	Impériale 6 L

The names of wines and their descriptions may seem confusing at first, but they are really very simple. Wine is usually identified by three or four things: the place where it was made, the type of grape that it was made from, the winery that produced it, and the year it was produced.

Take a look at the sample wine label below.

DOMESTIC WINE LABEL

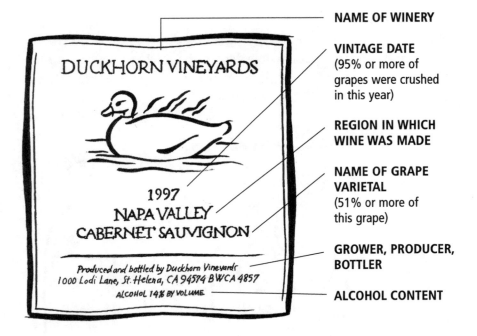

As indicated in the diagram, this wine was made in 1997, from Cabernet Sauvignon grapes, by Duckhorn Vineyards in Napa Valley, California.

Take a look at a different wine label, this one from France.

IMPORTED WINE LABEL

GENERAL REGION
IN WHICH WINE
WAS MADE

VINTAGE DATE
(95% or more of
grapes were crushed
in this year)

NAME OF WINERY

SPECIFIC REGION
IN WHICH WINE
WAS MADE

GROWER, PRODUCER,
BOTTLER

ALCOHOL CONTENT

IMPORTER

Things can get a bit confusing, because there is no industry standard for wine labels. European wines have historically been identified by the region in which they were produced, without identifying the type of grape. Rhône, Chianti, Bordeaux, and Burgundy are the names of famous wine-growing regions and also the names of the wines produced there. France, Italy, Germany, Spain, Chile, Australia, and South Africa, as well as the United States, all have identifiable wine-growing regions. Most American wines, and some wines from other countries, are primarily identified by the type of grape used to make them. Wines that are identified by the variety of grape used are known as *varietals.*

There are over four thousand varietals produced in the world today, but the average American wine consumer drinks wine made from fewer than ten different varieties of grape. What distinguishes these varietals from one another? Three things: appearance, smell, and taste.

Appearance

Appearance is an important aspect of wine, and one that is relatively easy to understand and identify. The *clarity, viscosity,* and *color* of a wine each add greatly to its overall appeal and to its drinkability.

Wines go through a process of clarification before they are sent to market. This process removes the bits of grape and other solids that are inevitably present when grapes are first mashed into juice. Some wine makers achieve *clarity* in their wines by simply holding new wines in large tanks until the solids settle to the bottom. Most high-volume wine makers use processes such as filtration, centrifugation, and flotation to clarify their wine. No matter what process is used, the end result is a wine with a clear appearance. Clarity, not cloudiness, is the desired appearance of any wine.

Viscosity can be defined as "ease of flow." Honey has a high degree of viscosity, while water has a low degree of viscosity. Wines differ in their viscosity depending on their alcohol content. Wine fans check the viscosity of a wine by looking at the wine as it wets the inside of a clean glass. The wine forms *tears,* or *legs,* down the inside of the glass as it drips back to the contents of the glass. The longer the legs, the higher the wine's alcohol content. Port wines (18 percent alcohol content) display long legs, while wines from Germany (11 percent alcohol content) will show almost no legs. Most table wines (12 to 14 percent alcohol content) exhibit viscosity somewhere in between.

Color is the most important element of a wine's appearance. Restaurants usually arrange their wine lists according to color, and guests often choose wine depending on the color.

The color of a wine is usually determined by two things: the color of the grape, and whether or not the grape skins were used in the wine-making process. Dark-skinned and red grapes make red wine. Light-colored grapes or grapes without their skins make white wines. White wines are not really white, but can range in color from light straw to amber. Rosé wines usually come from a blending of red and white wines. The French make their rosé wines from red grapes by allowing the red skins of the grapes to stay in the wine for a very short time to impart the distinctive rosé color.

As wines age, their color changes. The color comes from two sources in the grape: *tannins*, which stabilize color, and *anthocyan pigments*, which are the color agents themselves. Wines can gain or lose color as they age, depending on whether they have more tannins or more anthocyan pigments. Usually, white wines can be drunk younger than reds.

Smell and Taste

The smell of a wine is also called its *nose, aroma,* or *bouquet.* How a wine smells initially may be deceptive in determining taste, because it may take a little time for the rapidly dissipating odors to evaporate from a newly opened bottle of wine. But very often a wine's bouquet is as important to a guest as the way it tastes. Technically speaking, most wine flavors are actually aromas that are vaporized in the mouth and sensed through the back of the nasal passage. In the case of wine, smell and taste are really much the same.

Books have been filled with various descriptions of the ways different wines smell and taste. All you have to know is that drinking wine is an experience in search of a description. Wine drinkers try to describe the flavors of a wine in a poetic way that may at first seem ridiculous, but that actually can be quite accurate. Wines do indeed offer up a whole range of different flavors, and there are as many different ways to describe wine as there are flavors in wine.

Palate is a word that is used to refer to the taste of a wine. There are a wide variety of tastes that make up a wine's palate. You can notice the sweetness of a wine on the tip of your tongue. The opposite of a *sweet* wine is a *dry* wine. A wine that is slightly sweet is described as a *medium-dry* wine.

All wines have a certain amount of *acidity,* since acids, such as tartaric acids, exist in all grapes. Acidity is an important factor in judging white wines. White wines with just the right taste of acidity are described as *crisp,* or *tart.* If they do not have enough of an acid taste they are described as *fat,* or *flabby.*

The *body* of a wine is the impression that you get from the wine's overall taste. Wines that seem to be more flavorful than others are said to be *full-bodied.* Wines with a milder flavor are described as *light-bodied* or *medium-bodied.*

Tannin is a taste that is more common to red wines than white wines. Tannins are substances that exist naturally in grapes and grape skins. The tannin in red wines has a bitter taste. It is comparable to the acidity of a white wine. A red wine is described as *bitter* if there is too much tannin taste, and *firm* or *soft* if there is less tannin taste.

Dry, sweet, earth, peach, smoke, raspberry, hay, licorice. All these flavors and many more have been tasted in wines. There is no one correct vocabulary of wine. If you can describe the taste so that someone else says, "Yeah, that's right," then you've done a good job.

A wine's *balance* is the overall relationship of a wine's sweetness, tannin, acidity, flavor, and alcohol content. A *well-balanced* wine has all these ingredients in the right proportion. An *unbalanced* wine may be too sweet, too bitter (if there is too much tannin), or too acid. A wine with many elements of taste and smell is called a *complex* wine.

In addition to smell and taste, wine drinkers also talk about *texture,* the way the wine feels in the mouth. Wines are also described as *long* or *short,* depending on the time it takes for someone to experience the flavors and tastes of a particular wine. A wine's *finish* is how the mouth feels after the wine is drunk. It's almost a rule that great wines have a *long finish,* meaning that the flavor of the wine stays with the wine drinker long after the wine is drunk.

Study the wine chart on page 92 to learn the names of popular wines, as well as a little bit about their flavor and how they are to be served. Note that serving a wine chilled means serving it at about 50°F, which is not extremely cold. Also note that an *aperitif* [ah-pair-uh-TEEF] wine is a wine served as the first drink of a meal.

✳ REAL-WORLD EXPERIENCE ✳

 Uh-Oh The restaurant had a large and impressive wine selection. Unfortunately, our waitress was not familiar with the wines and seemed to become nervous when we began to ask questions about certain ones. She did not offer to send over another staff person who could help with our selection.

 Cheers Our waitress's knowledge of the wine list was impressive. She helped guide my companion to a perfect match of Pinot Grigio with a Parmesan chicken entrée. Her wine suggestion was proposed over a more-expensive first choice of the Chardonnay, which showed her concern for the dining experience and not just increasing the check. Great job!

Restaurant-goers who drink alcoholic beverages are drinking less these days, but drinking better liquors and wines. You can use this to your advantage by having a thorough knowledge of all the beverages your restaurant offers. Having a good working knowledge of the wine list is essential. The wine list details the wines offered by the restaurant. Many restaurants have extensive wine lists with as many as fifty to one hundred selections. While it may be impossible to be well versed on every bottle on the list, you should be able to make informed recommendations to the guests.

POPULAR WINES

TYPE	WINE	TASTE	PROPER SERVICE
Aperitif wines	Dry sherry, Dubonnet, Madeira, vermouth, white port	Dry to fruity	Serve before a meal, chilled.
Dessert wines	Muscat, Port, Sauternes, sherry, Sweet Marsala, Tokay	Sweet and heavy	Serve after a meal or with dessert, chilled or at room temperature.
White table wines	Chablis, Chardonnay, Riesling, Sauvignon Blanc	Dry to medium sweet	Serve before a meal or with food, chilled.
Rosé wines	Grenache rosé, white Zinfandel	Dry to medium sweet and fruity	Serve before a meal or with food, chilled.
Red table wines	Bordeaux, Burgundy, Cabernet Sauvignon, Merlot, Pinot Noir	Dry to medium dry	Serve with food, at room temperature.
Sparkling wines	Asti Spumante, Blanc de blancs, Blanc de noirs, champagne, prosecco	Very dry to sweet	Serve before a meal, chilled. Also for celebrations and toasts.

the Wine List

The wine list is a tool for you and the guest. A wine list should provide the full name of the wine and the year in which it was made. Note the names, prices, and general format on this sample list (continued on page 94).

Wines

SPARKLING / CHAMPAGNE

		🍷	🍾
NV	Domaine Chandon *Brut* NAPA	6.50	26.00
NV	Piper-Sonoma *Blanc de Noirs Brut* NAPA		36.00
NV	Taittinger *'La Francais' Brut* CHAMPAGNE		60.00
1995	Veuve Clicquot *Brut* CHAMPAGNE		105.00
1995	Perrier-Jouët *'Fleur de Champagne'* CHAMPAGNE		150.00

WHITES

Delightful Alternatives to Chardonnay

2000	Girard *Dry Chenin Blanc* NAPA		18.00
1999	King Estate *Pinot Gris* OREGON	5.50	22.00
1999	Albert Mann *Pinot Blanc Auxerrois* ALSACE		29.00
1999	Qupé Marsanne SANTA BARBARA		29.00
1999	Chalone *Pinot Blanc* CENTRAL COAST		32.00

Sauvignon Blanc / Fumé Blanc

2000	Chateau Ste. Michelle *Sauvignon Blanc* WASHINGTON		22.00
2000	Robert Pecota *Sauvignon Blanc* MONTERREY	6.50	26.00
1999	Honig *Sauvignon Blanc* NAPA		29.00
1998	Grgich Hills *Fumé Blanc* NAPA		36.00
2000	Cakebread *Sauvignon Blanc* NAPA		38.00

Chardonnay

2000	Quail Creek CALIFORNIA	5.50	22.00
2000	Beaulieu CARNEROS	7.50	30.00
2000	Sonoma-Cutrer SONOMA		33.00
1999	Hess Collection NAPA		40.00

Fruitier Wines

2000	Beringer *White Zinfandel* CALIFORNIA		18.00
2000	Field Stone *Gewürztraminer* SONOMA	6.00	24.00

Restaurants usually organize the wine list according to variety, price, and whether the wine is available by the glass or by the bottle. More and more restaurant-goers are ordering wine by the glass to accompany different courses of a meal.

Wines

REDS	🍷	🍾
Lighter, Smooth Reds		
1999 Pierre Chermette *Beaujolais (Unfiltered)* BURGUNDY	5.50	22.00
1998 Daniel Brusset CÔTES-DU-RHÔNE		24.00
1999 Rosemount *Shiraz* AUSTRALIA		24.00
1998 Rodano *Chianti Classico* TUSCANY		26.00
Pinot Noir		
NV Calera CALIFORNIA	6.50	26.00
1998 Bouchard Bourgogne BURGUNDY		28.00
1998 King Estate OREGON		30.00
1998 La Crema SONOMA		36.00
1999 Sanford SANTA BARBARA		48.00
Zinfandel		
1998 Peachy Canyon *'Bin 107'* PASO ROBLES	6.50	26.00
1998 Philip Staley DRY CREEK		30.00
1998 Dry Creek *'Old Vines'* SONOMA		33.00
1999 Frog's Leap NAPA		38.00
Merlot		
1999 Bogle CALIFORNIA	5.50	22.00
1998 Hogue Cellars WASHINGTON	7.00	28.00
1998 Pine Ridge NAPA		36.00
1998 Cuvaison CARNEROS-NAPA		55.00
1997 Château Belgrave POMEROL-BORDEAUX		80.00
Cabernet Sauvignon / Meritage		
1997 Sebastiani *'Sonoma Cask'* SONOMA	6.00	24.00
1998 La Jolla *Grand Reserve* CHILE		26.00
1997 Chateau Ste. Michelle WASHINGTON		28.00
1998 David Wynn AUSTRALIA		30.00
1998 Honig NAPA		48.00
1997 Hess Collection NAPA		52.00
1997 Jordan ALEXANDER VALLEY		85.00

Many wine lists are organized by the region or country from which the wines come. Talk with the person who puts together the restaurant's wine list to learn what is what. And be sure to attend staff wine meetings and tastings. You will learn the most valuable information about your wine list from discussing the various wines and wine and food pairings with your coworkers.

Matching Food and Wine

Wines are best enjoyed with food. The taste of food can change the taste of a particular wine, and vice versa. The key to good wine service is to recommend wines that will complement a particular food.

Think of wine as a seasoning, something that affects the flavor of food. A big wine with a strong flavor will usually go well with flavorful food. If the food does not have a strong taste, a more subtle wine may be appropriate. You don't want to drink a subtle wine with strongly flavored food, because the taste of the food will overpower the taste of the wine.

✳ CLASSIC FOOD AND WINE PAIRINGS ✳

MILD-FLAVORED FOOD	LIGHT-BODIED WINE
Oysters	Chablis
Roast chicken	Chianti
MEDIUM-FLAVORED FOOD	MEDIUM-BODIED WINE
Shrimp	White Graves
Pork chops	Merlot
FULL-FLAVORED FOOD	FULL-BODIED WINE
Salmon	Puligny-Montrachet
Sirloin steak	Cabernet Sauvignon

Try to match the characteristics of the wine and the food. The only way to know what wine goes with what food is to try it, or to have someone you trust tell you. Describe the characteristics of the wines for your guests. When suggesting wine, stress benefits not features. If a guest raves about a certain wine, remember it, and suggest the wine to others.

Many people still think that white wine must be paired with white meat and red wine with red meat. But this is not necessarily true. A red wine like Pinot Noir might be a great substitute for a white wine on certain occasions. If you sense that your guests appreciate wine and know something about it, make a suggestion that is out of the ordinary. They will remember it—as long as it's a good suggestion.

Wine Service

Proper wine service begins with helping the guest make a choice. If you see people staring at the wine list in confusion, they are probably not sophisticated about wine. Ask them if they want a red wine or a white wine. Then ask them if they like a sweet wine or a dry wine. Then recommend a few selections from the wine list. If a guest places an order for a food item without ordering a bottle of wine, suggest a wine that would go with the food item.

Sometimes a guest will bring a bottle of wine to a restaurant. It may be a special wine to celebrate an occasion, or a gift to one of the other people in that party. If you see that a guest has brought a bottle of wine, offer to open it. If the guests wish to drink the wine with their entrées, offer to store the wine or chill it if it needs to be served chilled. Bring the wine to the table at the proper time, open the bottle and pour it (see pages 98 and 99 for instructions). Restaurants usually charge a *corkage fee* for this service.

If the guest orders a bottle of wine, show the wine to him or her to confirm the selection, open the bottle, pour a little to taste, wait for approval, then fill the glasses. That's basically all there is to it.

Wineglasses

Some restaurants use particular glasses for particular types of wine. Know which glasses go with which wines and make sure you have the correct glass before serving the wine. There are three main types of wineglasses:

- Flutes for champagne and other sparkling wines (tall and thin)
- Wineglasses for red wine (larger, more rounded bowl)
- Wineglasses for white wine (tulip-shaped bowl)

The shape of a wineglass can affect the taste of the wine, which is the reason why different types of wine are served in different glasses. Glasses for red wine often have a wider opening at the mouth than glasses for white wine. This lets air reach the red wine more easily, allowing for the dissipation of any acidic flavors and also allowing the red wine's bouquet or aroma to open up. Always hold any type of glass by the stem, not the bowl. This keeps fingerprints off the bowl and keeps your hand from heating the wine.

Not only do glasses come in different shapes, but they range in size as well. A good all-purpose wineglass should have a minimum capacity of 10 ounces.

STANDARD WINE GLASSWARE

Champagne flutes   Red wineglasses   White wineglasses

Step-by-Step Wine Service

When serving an older wine, remove the bottle from the wine rack (also called a wine bin) gently, which will allow any sediment in red wine to tumble to the bottom of the bottle. Red wines should be served at room temperature, about 65°F. White wines should be chilled to about 50°F. Ask the guests if they want white wine put in an ice bucket. If they do, bring one.

Present the bottle from the right of the person who ordered it. Hold the bottle in the palm of your hand at a 45-degree angle with the label out. Allow your guest to look at the label and tell you that yes, indeed, it is the wine he or she ordered. Read the name and the vintage out loud, to make sure there is no mistake.

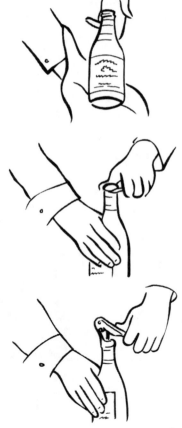

On approval, open the bottle. With some practice, you will be able to open a bottle of wine with one hand while holding it in the other. Some restaurants will allow you to put the wine bottle down on a corner of the table on a coaster or a plate before opening it, but most require you to open the wine bottle in the air. Be careful when opening an older bottle of red wine this way, as the sediments will swirl up from the bottom.

Step 1: Cut the foil below the lower lip with a complete, neat cut, using the blade on your corkscrew. Put the foil in your pocket.

Step 2: Sink the corkscrew in the middle of the cork to make sure it goes down the center of the cork. Twist the corkscrew all the way into the cork, or as far as it will go with the lever on the rim of the bottle.

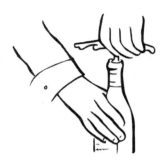

Step 3: Grasp the edge of the lever and the neck of the bottle firmly with one hand. With the other hand, pull up on the handle of the corkscrew with a firm, continuous motion. When the cork is removed, wipe inside the lip of the bottle with a napkin to remove any bits of cork or sediment. Some people believe that the cork indicates the condition of the wine; other people think this is nonsense. To avoid any trouble, place the cork to the right of the host and pour an ounce or two for tasting. Stand back to the host's right and make sure he or she can read the label.

Step 4: After the host tastes the wine and accepts it, pour the wine quickly and efficiently from each guest's right. Make sure the neck of the bottle is an inch or two above the glass, and avoid touching the bottle to the rim of the glass. The label of the bottle should face out from your palm. Fill the glasses no more than half full, and make sure that all the glasses around the table are filled to the same level. As each glass is filled, give a half-turn of the bottle while raising the neck upwards. Use a napkin to catch any wine that dribbles down the neck of the bottle. If serving a couple, pour for the non-taster first. In a group, move clockwise around the table, serving women first, then men. If there are eight or more in the group, just go clockwise. Always pour so that a woman finishes the bottle.

Step 5: Put the bottle back on the table to the right of the host, with the label visible.

Decanting

Some restaurants open a bottle of wine and pour it into a container called a *decanter* before it is served. This process is called *decanting*. Wines are decanted in order to let the wine *breathe,* or absorb oxygen. This allows the flavors in a wine to develop. Breathing also allows any off odors in the wine to dissipate. Decanting can also help to remove particles and sediment from older bottles of wine.

Decanting is a somewhat controversial operation. Most white wines do not need decanting. Young red wines actually taste better after decanting because their tannins soften and the wine's flavor becomes less harsh. One hour is long enough to let most young red wines aerate or breathe although a few minutes may be enough for certain tannin tastes to soften.

Some older red wines develop sediment, or particles in the wine that solidify over time and fall to the bottom of the bottle. Decanting a wine allows the server to remove the sediment from a bottle of wine. The trick here is to stop pouring the wine into the decanter before you reach the sediment. Older wines with sediment will lose flavor if left to breathe for too long; as you learn about wines you'll develop knowledge about how long to let different wines breathe.

Port is another wine that benefits from decanting and breathing. But since decanting is a controversial process for wine-lovers, talk with your sommelier or another wine-savvy coworker before you take the trouble to decant a wine before serving, unless your restaurant policy is different.

TYPES OF CORKSCREWS

Ashwood-handled corkscrew

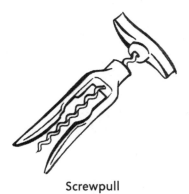

Screwpull

Butterfly

Two-pronged extractor

Waiter's tool

Step-by-Step Champagne Service

Be careful when opening champagne, which is from the Champagne region of France, and other sparkling wines. Sparkling wines contain trapped gasses, and these gasses are under such a great amount of pressure that the cork on the bottle is wired on. You can injure yourself or others if you don't open a bottle of sparkling wine correctly. Sparkling wine should be served quite cold, at 42°F. Use an ice bucket and ask the guests if they want to continue chilling the wine. Do not shake the bottle when bringing it to the table. This will cause the pressure to intensify and the wine to foam after opening.

Before opening, use a service napkin to dry the bottle, and present the bottle to the host, holding it at a 45-degree angle.

Step 1: Remove the foil from the top of the bottle. The cork will be covered by wire.

Step 2: Locate the wire loop and untwist it, loosening the wires. As you remove the wire, quickly place your thumb on top of the cork. This will help to prevent the cork from accidentally popping off the bottle.

Step 3: Place a service napkin over the cork, leaving a little slack between the napkin and the cork. Remove your thumb.

Step 4: Holding the bottle at a 45-degree angle, grasp the cork and slowly twist the bottle. Make sure that you do not have the bottle pointed at anyone or at any mirrors or windows. As you slowly twist the bottle, you will feel the cork starting to loosen. Keep slowly twisting the bottle until the cork slides out. The service napkin will catch the cork as it is released from the bottle. It should make a pleasant gasping noise as it is released, rather than popping.

Step 5: Continue to hold the bottle at a 45-degree angle to allow the pressure to equalize. Sparkling wine is poured twice. The first pour will foam in the glass. As the foam subsides, pour again to fill the glass. As always, serve women first.

~s, tables will order more than one bottle of wine. If they
~ing another bottle of the same wine, place a fresh wine-
~fore the host. Open the bottle and pour a small amount of
the wine into the fresh glass so that the host may approve the second bottle. Once the host approves of the bottle, refill each guest's
wineglass. Remove the tasting glass.

If the table orders a different wine for their second bottle, you
must bring every guest a fresh glass. Some guests may want more
wine, but not a whole bottle. This is an opportunity to sell wine by
the glass. Suggest a wine to complement the guests' entrées.

Wine by the Glass

Many restaurants are offering more wines by the glass or by the half
carafe. Offering a wide selection of wines by the glass or by the
half carafe allows guests to:

- Drink better wine without having to order a full bottle
- Taste different wines and broaden their wine perspective
- Solve the problem of "She wants white wine, I want red"
- Match wines to their food

Handling Complaints

Sometimes a guest will reject a bottle of wine. When this happens,
apologize and prepare to bring a new bottle of wine. In some cases,
the wine is *corked,* meaning that the bottle had a faulty cork and the
wine spoiled. It is easy to tell when a wine is corked—it tastes like
vinegar. Save the cork to return to the wholesaler for credit.

Wines are very rarely corked; most guests return a wine simply because they do not like the taste or the smell, though nothing
is really wrong with the wine. Sometimes a guest will smell a wine
directly after it has been poured and will reject it because of what
he or she thinks is a bad odor.

In many cases, the wine may not actually be bad. The guest may instead be smelling the sulfur dioxide in the wine or the tannins, which take time to dissipate. Never argue with a guest, but you may wish to call the manager or the sommelier to explain the situation. If the wine is rejected, take time to taste it yourself away from the table. Tasting bad wine is a good wine-learning experience.

In summary, proper table service demands that you know a red and a white wine that will go with every dish on the menu. You also must have a favorite white, red, and sparkling wine on the wine list that you can talk about intelligently.

If you enjoy wine, take the time to improve your wine knowledge. Read a wine book. Talk with your coworkers. Spring for a bottle of good wine on occasion, drink it, describe it, and talk about what foods it would complement. Test yourself on the types of wine you have drunk and the types of flavors you remember.

A good way to learn about wines is to keep a tasting notebook. In your notebook, write the name and vintage of the wine, what flavors you tasted, and why you did or did not like it. Some other ways to learn about wine include:

- Subscribing to *Wine Spectator* magazine.
- Getting feedback from your guests who drink wine by asking them what they liked or disliked about the wine
- Talking to your coworkers about wine
- Asking questions of your wine buyer and wine salespeople
- Developing an understanding of how and why certain wines complement different foods
- Reading books about wine, including *Oz Clarke's New Encyclopedia of Wine* by Oz Clarke (Webster's International Publishers Limited), and *Wine for Dummies* by Ed McCarthy et al. (Hungry Minds Inc.)

These will help you to become an excellent wine salesperson and improve your guests' dining experience. To get a start on improving your wine knowledge, study the following glossary of wine terms.

WINE GLOSSARY

Alsace [al-SASS]: A wine-producing region on the eastern border of France, famous for its white wines.

Aperitif [ah-pair-uh-TEEF]: The first drink offered at a meal.

Appellation (short for *appellation d'origine contrôlée*): A French term for the system of designating and controlling geographically based names of wines and spirits, such as Champagne.

Aroma: The scent, or smell, of a wine based on the grape variety, fermentation, and aging. *See also* Bouquet.

Barbaresco: A strong red wine made from Nebbiolo grapes grown near the village of Barbaresco in northwest Italy.

Barbera: A red grape, one of the most popular planted in Italy.

Barolo: A Nebbiolo grape grown near the village of Barolo in northwest Italy.

Beaujolais [bo-zho-LAY]: A fruity, light-bodied red wine made from Gamay grapes, produced in the Beaujolais region of France.

Bordeaux [bore-DOE]: Red and white wines, ranging in flavor from light and fruity to strong, produced in the Bordeaux region of France.

Bouquet: The scent, or smell, of a wine developed through fermentation and aging. *See also* Aroma.

Burgundy: Red and white wines, produced in the Burgundy region of France. The name is also given to some wines made in the United States.

Cabernet Franc [KA-behr-nay FRAHNK]: A black grape variety grown in France.

Cabernet Sauvignon [KA-behr-nay SOH-vee-nyawn]: The most popular red wine grape, grown in many parts of the world.

Cellar: A collection of wine, as well as the place in which wine is stored. Also called a *cave* in French, a *cantina* in Italian, and a *bodega* in Spanish.

Chablis [shah-BLEE]: A white wine, fruity in flavor, made from Chardonnay grapes in the Chablis region of France. The name is also given to some wines made in the United States.

Champagne [sham-PAIN]: Sparkling wine made in the Champagne region of France. The name is also given to some sparkling wines made in the United States using the same bottling method.

Chardonnay [shar-doh-NAY]: A variety of white grape originally grown in France.

Chenin Blanc [SHEH-nin BLAWNK]: A white wine grape with a dry, fruity flavor.

Chianti [key-AHN-tee]: A red wine from the Chianti region of Italy.

Claret [KLAR-eht]: A word used to describe red wines from the Bordeaux region of France.

Cru [KROO]: The French term for a high-quality vineyard.

Cuvé [koo-VAY]: The French term for vat, or tank.

Decanting: The process of serving wine by pouring it from the bottle into another container called a decanter (see page 100).

Filtering: The process by which solid particles are strained out of some wines using various sorts of filters.

Fumé Blanc [fu-MAY blahnk]: Another name for the Sauvignon Blanc grape.

Gewürztraminer [ge-VURTZ-tra-MEE-ner]: A white wine grape with a dry to semisweet spicy taste.

House wine: The wine served by a restaurant if the guest does not request a particular type of wine.

Loire [LWAHR]: A wine-growing region along the Loire River in France.

Malbec [mahl-BEHK]: A black grape grown in the Bordeaux region of France and in Argentina.

Meritage [MEHR-ih-tihj]: A trademarked name for U.S. wines made by blending several grape varieties.

Merlot [mare-LOW]: A red wine grape with a smooth flavor.

Montepulciano [mon-tay-pul-chee-AH-no]: A red grape variety common to central Italy.

Muscat [MUS-kat]: A grape used to make dessert wine and sparkling wine.

Nebbiolo [neh-BYOH-loh]: A black grape from northwest Italy.

Petite Sirah [pe-TEE si-RAH]: A black grape grown in North and South America.

Piedmont: A wine region in northwest Italy.

Pinot Blanc [PEE-noh BLAWNK]: A white wine grape with a dry, fruity taste.

Pinot Grigio [PEE-noh GREE-gee-oh] or **Pinot Gris** [PEE-noh GREE]: A popular white wine produced in Italy and France.

Pinot Noir [PEE-noh NWAHR]: A red wine grape with a rich, fruity taste.

Port: A red or white fortified wine, traditionally made in Portugal.

Provence [pro-VANZ]: A wine-producing region in the southeast of France.

Rhône: A wine-growing region along the Rhône River in France.

Riesling [REEZ-ling]: A white wine grape with a sweet, fruity taste.

Sangiovese [san-joh-VAY-say]: A variety of red grape that is the most popular type planted in Italy.

Sauternes [soh-TURN]: A white wine with a sweet taste, produced from Semillon grapes in the Bordeaux region of France.

Sauvignon Blanc [SOH-vee-nyawn BLAHNK]: A white wine grape with a fresh taste, sometimes called Fumé Blanc in the United States.

Sec [SEHK]: The French word for "dry."

Sherry: A fortified wine. Dry sherry may be served chilled before a meal; sweet sherry may be served at room temperature at the end of a meal.

Syrah [su-RAH]: One of the most popular black grape varieties.

Table wine: A term used to distinguish wines of ordinary alcoholic strength from fortified wines. Most table wines are between 9 and 15 percent alcohol.

Tannins: A group of chemicals present in the skin of red grapes that add bitterness to the taste of wine.

Tokay: The name of a popular Hungarian wine, also called Tokaji.

Tuscany: An important wine-growing region in central Italy.

Varietal: A wine named for the grape from which it is made.

Vintage: The year in which a wine was made.

Zinfandel [ZIN-fan-del]: A red wine grape with a fruity taste, grown in California. Used to make red wine as well as a rosé called white Zinfandel.

"After years of being intimidated by selling wine, I decided to do something about it. I bought Wine for Dummies *and learned the basics and more. Now I'm rereading it for the third time and can navigate my way around any wine list."*

CHAPTER 8

All About Food

A broad knowledge of food is one of the most important keys to success for any wait person. After all, guests come to your restaurant to enjoy food served to them properly. Since food is the product you are selling, the better you know food, and the more familiar you are with ingredients and cooking techniques, the better able you will be to provide your guests with a rewarding food experience. If you are enthusiastic about food, your guests will sense your enthusiasm and will take a special interest in the foods and dishes offered by your restaurant. Your knowledge of food will help transform your guests' experience from just another dinner to an exciting culinary adventure.

We have already introduced the importance of being familiar with your restaurant's menu, and we have discussed the importance of using the proper vocabulary when describing menu items (see chapter 3). This chapter will give you a more detailed understanding of foods and food preparation. Remember that it is important for you to know the ingredients in each dish you serve. Not only will this help you guide your guests' menu choices, but a thorough knowledge of ingredients is also necessary because of guests' allergies and dietary restrictions (see pages 31 and 32). Certain people are so allergic that they might die if they are exposed to the wrong foods. So, if a guest asks if a certain dish contains a certain ingredient, do not guess. If you don't know the answer, ask the chef or manager.

Become familiar with the foods described in this chapter. As you get to know various foods and cooking styles, you will better appreciate the unique flavors created by different ingredients and cooking techniques. This chapter will familiarize you with various dishes, food items, and preparation and cooking terms that appear on menus these days.

ON YOUR OWN

Go to a restaurant and order an entrée. Then write down all the ingredients you taste. After you have finished eating, compliment the waitperson on the meal, then take a few minutes to discuss the ingredients. Make a note of how many ingredients you correctly identify. As your *palate*, or tasting ability, develops, you will improve your understanding and appreciation of diverse cuisines.

Meat

Whether it's beef, veal, lamb, pork, or poultry, meat is animal muscle. As the proteins in the muscle cook, they become drier and shrink. Chefs know that careful control of this process is the difference between a tender, juicy serving of meat and a dry, tough one.

CUTS OF BEEF

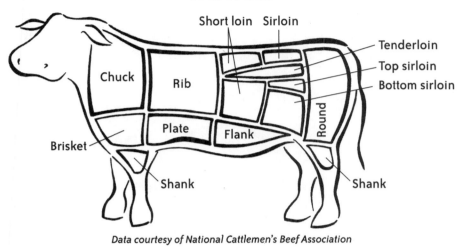

Data courtesy of National Cattlemen's Beef Association

Beef

Sirloin, tenderloin, prime rib, New York strip, rib-eye, T-bone—beef is an American favorite and a menu mainstay in today's restaurants. Beef is meat taken from cattle. Typically, the meat from a younger animal is very tender but less flavorful than the meat from an older animal. The best meat for quality and flavor comes from an animal that is a year and a half to two years old. It is important for you to know the most popular cuts of beef and which cuts are restaurant favorites.

You will hear terms that refer to different grades, or qualities, of beef. There are eight grades of beef, although you need to be concerned only with three of them—*prime, choice,* and *select.* Some factors used to determine the quality of the beef are the proportion of meat to bone and the proportion of fat to lean. High quality beef has a high degree of *marbling,* meaning thin lines of fat running through the muscle. As a general rule, the more marbling in a cut of beef, the more flavor. Prime is the highest quality beef, choice is the second highest quality, and select is the third highest quality. Although less than 2 percent of all graded beef is prime, restaurants generally serve prime grade beef. Because it is the highest quality beef, prime is sold at the highest price of all grades of beef.

You will also hear the term *aging* in regard to steaks. Aging is the process of keeping beef at refrigerated temperatures for a specific amount of time to optimize tenderness and flavor. Aging increases the quality of the meat and therefore the price.

BEEF QUALITY GRADES

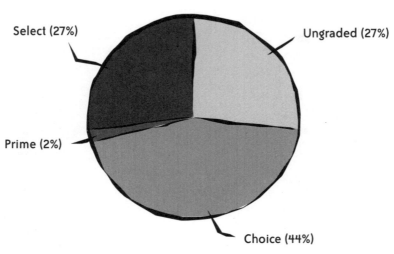

Select (27%)

Ungraded (27%)

Prime (2%)

Choice (44%)

Data courtesy of National Cattlemen's Beef Association

STEAKS AND ROASTS

As a knowledgeable waitperson, you need to know the different cuts of beef. *Steaks* and *roasts* are cuts of beef. Steaks are flat cuts, usually one to two inches thick. Roasts are much thicker cuts. Carefully study the most popular cuts listed below.

Filet mignon [fu-LAY min-YAWN]: An extremely tender cut of beef from the small end of the tenderloin. It has little or no marbling, thus making the meat less flavorful than other cuts of beef, but the tender texture makes it a very popular selection.

New York strip: A steak cut from the loin. Some marbling.

Prime rib: A roast that contain the ribs and the rib-eye, cut from the ribs. Often slow roasted and very flavorful.

Rib-eye: A steak cut from the center of the rib. Very tender and flavorful with good marbling.

Sirloin: Tender or tough beef that can be cut into roasts or steaks. Little marbling.

T-bone: A steak cut from the loin that contains part of the New York strip. Good marbling, very flavorful; also called a porterhouse.

Steaks are usually prepared to a guest's specifications—*rare, medium-rare, medium, medium-well,* or *well done.* Use this guide to familiarize yourself with the temperatures, colors, and textures of these different degrees of doneness.

Doneness	Internal Temp.	Internal Color	External Texture
Rare	125°F	Red	Feel of your cheek
Medium-Rare	135°F	Warm red	Feel of your chin
Medium	140°F	Warm pink	Feel of the tip of your nose
Medium-Well	145°F	No pink	Feel of your forehead above the nose
Well Done	150°F	Gray	Feel of a shoe sole

Restaurant-goers are quite particular about how their steaks are cooked. Get to know how your chef prepares steak and talk with your guests about how they want their steak prepared. For example, if well done means cooked until there is no moisture, explain that to your guests. Be sure to check with a guest a few minutes after serving a steak to make sure the steak is prepared to his or her liking.

VEAL

Veal is meat taken from a young calf. It is delicate and pale and is usually at its best in the spring and late winter. Milk-fed veal is meat taken from calves that have not been weaned and have only had their mother's milk. There are many dishes made with veal.

Osso bucco [OH-soh BOO-koh]: An Italian dish made of veal shanks cooked with ingredients similar to veal Marengo (olive oil, white wine, onions, tomatoes, garlic, and so on). Additional stock of some kind, anchovies, carrots, celery, and lemon peel are also added, and it is served with risotto or polenta.

Veal cordon bleu [kor-dohn-BLUH]: A French dish made with thin slices of veal, prosciutto or ham, and Gruyère or another Swiss cheese. The cheese and meat are stacked in layers, breaded, and sautéed until golden brown.

Veal Marengo [muh-RENG-goh]: An Italian dish made by sautéing veal in olive oil to give it some color and then braising it with other ingredients, some of which are garlic, onions, white wine, and tomatoes.

Veal Orloff [OR-lawf]: A French dish that is prepared with braised loin of veal slices spread with mushrooms and onions that have been sautéed. These slices are tied together to reform the veal loin. It is covered with more mushrooms and onions and topped with a béchamel sauce and some grated Parmesan cheese. Then the reformed loin is browned in an oven.

Veal Oscar: A Swedish dish made from veal, crab, crawfish, and asparagus. It is prepared and covered with béarnaise sauce. It was created and named for King Oscar II because he loved all of its ingredients.

Veal parmigiana [pahr-muh-ZHAH-nuh]: An Italian dish made from veal slices dipped in egg, milk, grated Parmesan cheese, and seasoned breadcrumbs. They are sautéed and covered with a tomato-based sauce.

Veal picatta [pih-KAH-tuh]: Another Italian dish made by dredging slices of veal in seasoned flour and quickly sautéing them. A sauce made from the pan drippings, lemon juice, and chopped parsley is poured over them.

Veal scallopini [skah-luh-PEE-nee]: An Italian dish prepared like veal picatta but served with a sauce made with wine and tomatoes.

OTHER BEEF TERMS

Corned beef: Beef brisket flavored with spices and salt.

Sweetbreads: The thymus gland of young cows, calves, pigs, or lambs.

Tartare [tar-TAR]: A dish made of ground, very high-quality raw lean beef. It is served in a mound with a raw egg on top. Some typical accompaniments are chopped raw onions, capers, and parsley. Beef tartare is sometimes referred to as steak tartare.

Tripe: The stomach lining of a cow. Menudo is a popular Mexican tripe stew.

Lamb

Lamb is meat taken from a baby sheep usually less than 12 months old. Like veal, lamb is known for its tender, succulent meat and is rated *prime, choice,* and *good.* It can be cut and prepared in steaks, chops, or roasts, and it is most often served medium-rare, but some guests may prefer it medium or well done. A rack of lamb is 8 lamb ribs cut as one piece of meat and is typically prepared by roasting it in the oven. Lamb is becoming more popular, although it is still not nearly as popular as beef.

CUTS OF LAMB

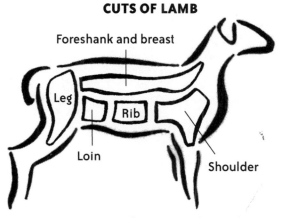

Data courtesy of American Lamb Council

115

Pork

Pork, the meat taken from a hog or pig, can be prepared in almost any way; it can be roasted, grilled, sautéed, panfried, or stir-fried. The pork sold now is much more nutritious than in the past; it has less fat, fewer calories, and less cholesterol. Pork has a truly subtle flavor, can be combined with many varied seasonings, and is used in dishes from most cuisines. Pork must be cooked before serving, because the meat in its raw state may contain parasites that can cause illness in humans. Some guests may not realize that pork is completely safe when cooked to a medium doneness even when there is a hint of pink in the center.

The most popular cuts of fresh pork are cut from the loin, the meat that runs on either side of the backbone. These cuts include the ribs, chops, loin, and tenderloin. Pork can also be cured, or flavored by smoking or drying.

CUTS OF PORK

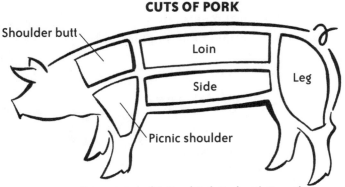

Data courtesy of National Pork Producer's Council

OTHER PORK TERMS

Bacon: Thin strips of pork from the side of the pig, salted and sometimes smoked.

Chorizo [chor-EE-zoh, chor-EE-soh]: A Mexican fresh pork sausage flavored with garlic, chile powder, and other spices. A Spanish version uses smoked pork. The meat is coarsely ground. Chorizo is usually sautéed and added as an ingredient in other dishes.

Ham: A cut of pork usually taken from the leg.

Pancetta [pan-CHEH-tuh]: An Italian bacon. It is not smoked and is used to flavor other dishes.

Proscuitto [proh-SHOO-toh]: A ham produced in Parma, Italy. It comes from pigs weighing at least 308 pounds and slaughtered at age ten months. Proscuitto is cut into paper-thin slices, and is often served as an appetizer.

Spareribs: A delicious, fatty cut of pork taken from the ribs of a pig. It is usually marinated and barbecued.

Poultry

Poultry is the general term for chickens, ducks, geese, quails, and other domestic birds. Some birds served at restaurants are hunted in the wild and are referred to as game birds or game fowl. Because poultry is relatively healthful, inexpensive, and easy to prepare, it is popular in cuisines all over the world.

CHICKEN

Chicken is very popular on restaurant menus. It is low in fat and calories, and its delicate flavor adapts well to seasonings, sauces, and different methods of preparation. Chefs enjoy cooking chicken because it allows them creative freedom, and chicken is a popular item in almost any cuisine.

Chickens are usually rated by their size and age. The older the chicken the tougher the meat, but the more flavorful when cooked. Fryer, broiler, roaster, and stewing chicken are some terms used to describe types of bird. Fresh chicken is available as cut-up parts, boned and skinned, or whole. The most popular parts of the chicken are the breast, thighs, wings, and legs (drumsticks). Giblets are the liver, heart, and gizzard of chicken and other types of poultry.

Several other types of chicken are also served by restaurants. A capon is a castrated rooster and averages about 7 pounds. Capons are usually roasted, and although they are flavorful, they're not very popular. A Rock Cornish game hen is a small chicken, generally weighing about one pound, that is also often served roasted. In a restaurant, one is usually served per guest.

OTHER BIRDS

Duck: Both wild and domesticated ducks are served in restaurants. Wild ducks tend to be slightly tougher than the domesticated variety. Duck is usually roasted.

Goose: Larger than the chicken or the duck, the goose is a female bird. The male is the gander. Goose is more commonly served in Europe, where is it usually roasted. Foie gras [fwah GRAH] is a special dish made from the enlarged liver of a goose or duck.

Guinea hen: Similar to chicken, but much more flavorful. Usually served roasted.

Quail: A small bird found both in the wild and domesticated. Quail is usually served roasted, two birds per serving.

Squab: A farm-raised pigeon that has not yet flown and is slaughtered at the age of 4 weeks.

Turkey: A domesticated bird, much larger than the chicken, that is indigenous to North America. Turkeys are usually smoked or roasted, although Cajun deep-fried turkey is also becoming popular. Like chicken, the most popular parts of the turkey are the breast and legs.

Fish and Shellfish

Fish is a popular and adaptable restaurant food that is served broiled, baked, poached, grilled, blackened, sautéed, panfried, or even raw. Fish can be gutted and served whole, or cut into steaks or fillets. Fish steaks are cut from large fish, crosswise, into thick slices. Fillets are boneless pieces of fish cut from the side and away from the backbone.

It is important to know how to describe the fish items on the menu. Guests want to know if a particular fish is delicate, mild, firm, fine, dense, or chewy.

Cutting a fish into steaks

Filleting a fish

Freshwater Fish

Freshwater fish live in freshwater rivers or lakes. They generally have lots of fine bones, which can make eating them somewhat tricky. The most popular types of freshwater fish include bass, catfish, pike, and trout. Catfish today are usually farm raised. The flesh is firm and mild in flavor. Pike is firm and lean. It can be filleted or cut into steaks. Trout is a very well known freshwater fish. It is firm-textured and has a higher fat content than pike. Trout is usually served whole, and popular types include rainbow, brown, and lake trout.

Catfish   Rainbow trout

Saltwater Fish

Saltwater fish, generically known as seafood (along with saltwater shellfish), live in the salt water of oceans, bays, and seas. Saltwater fish can be prepared in many of the same ways as freshwater fish, either whole, as steaks, or as fillets. However, many saltwater fish are much larger than freshwater fish, and are more likely to be served as steaks.

The meat of each type of saltwater fish has a distinct taste, texture, and appearance. Some of these differences are subtle and require

119

tasting the different varieties of fish, but the general characteristics of some of the popular varieties of saltwater fish are listed below.

Cod: A firm, lean fish with a mild flavor.

Flounder: A fine-textured fish with a delicate flavor.

Haddock [HAD-uhk]: A fish with a firm texture and a mild flavor, related to cod.

Halibut [HAL-uh-buht]: A fish with meat that is firm, mild flavored, and low in fat.

Mahi-mahi: The Hawaiian term for dolphinfish, which has a sweet, pink, firm flesh that turns white when cooked.

Orange roughy [RUHF-ee]: A low-fat fish with firm, white flesh and a mild flavor.

Redfish: A firm-textured, low-fat fish; also called *red snapper.*

Rockfish: A low-fat, firm-fleshed fish.

Salmon [SAM-uhn]: A pink, soft-textured fish with a high fat content. Salmon live in salt water, but breeds in fresh water.

Sea bass: A fish that is lean to moderately fat, firm, and with a delicate flavor.

Shark: A flavorful, low-fat fish with dense meat.

Sole: A fish with a delicate flavor and fine, firm-textured meat.

Swordfish: A mild-flavored fish with moderately fat, firm, and dense meat.

Tuna: A rich-flavored fish with a moderate to high fat content and a firm texture.

Winter flounder

Silver salmon

Shellfish

Most shellfish live in salt water. Some shellfish grow wild, but much of the shellfish served in restaurants is raised on farms. There are two main kinds of shellfish: mollusks and crustaceans.

MOLLUSKS

Mollusks have three body regions: the head, the body, and the "foot." They usually, but not always, have a shell. The edible land snail is a peculiar type of mollusk that is popular in French cuisine. The most popular sea mollusks sold in restaurants fall into two categories: bivalves and cephalopods.

Bivalves: All bivalves have two shells. Well-known bivalves include clams, mussels, oysters, and scallops. There are dozens of types of clams, some eaten raw and some cooked. Soft-shell clams include the common steamers, and they are steamed, deep-fried, or used in soups or chowders. Hard-shell clams can be eaten raw, sautéed, steamed, or grilled in their shells. Littleneck clams are hard-shell clams often eaten raw on the half shell. Scallops can be eaten raw, but usually they are steamed or sautéed before serving. Oysters are often eaten raw. Restaurants have to be careful when serving oysters. Bad oysters carry bacteria that can make people seriously ill. A good guideline is to serve oysters only during the months that have an "r" in them (September through April). The risk from bacteria is higher in the summer months. In addition to serving them raw, oysters can also be served fried, grilled, or used in stews and soups.

Cephalopods: Mollusks such as squid and octopus are cephalopods. Squid has a sweet, nutty flavor. It is often served deep-fried or sautéed lightly. Octopus must be precooked to tenderize it. After precooking, it can be grilled or stewed.

Squid

121

CRUSTACEANS

In the crustacean category, you'll find some of the most popular seafood selections, including crab, crawfish, lobster, and shrimp.

Crab: The second most popular crustacean (after shrimp) served in restaurants in the United States. Crabs are noted for their sweet, succulent meat. Some of the most common crab species are blue crab, king crab, snow crab, Dungeness crab, and stone crab. Live crabs are boiled or steamed. Soft-shell crabs are crabs that have shed their hard shell. Caught before they develop a new, hard shell, soft-shell crabs can be eaten shell and all and are served deep-fried, sautéed, or grilled. In the United States, the blue crab (found along the Atlantic and Gulf Coasts) is the species most commonly eaten in its soft-shell state. Crabmeat is used in crab cakes, sauces, salads, and stir-fries.

Crawfish: A freshwater crustacean that looks like a miniature lobster. The best cooking technique for live crawfish is boiling or steaming. The meat of the tail is used in a number of dishes, including the Southern dishes crawfish bisque and crawfish étoufée.

Lobster: A sweet, delectable crustacean. Lobsters fall into two groups: those with edible claws, usually called Maine lobsters, and those without edible claws but with excellent tail meat. Serving whole lobster in restaurants requires a special fork and claw crackers in order for the guest to get the meat out of the claws. Sometimes a bib is supplied to protect the guest's clothing, and a finger bowl or moist towel is needed to clean fingers after the meal.

Shrimp: The most popular of all seafood sold in restaurants. Some types of shrimp include gulf white, Mexican white, gulf pink, and black tiger. Gulf white have pale shells and can be very large. Mexican white are usually farm-raised and are similar to gulf white. Gulf pink, or brown shrimp, are a smaller wild variety. Black tiger are the most common shrimp, farm-raised, with gray shells. A prawn is a crustacean that resembles a small lobster, but the term is also used to refer to a large shrimp.

Black tiger shrimp

Fruits, Vegetables, and Legumes

Fresh fruits and vegetables have come a long way as menu items and ingredients over the last few years, and there's an ever-growing assortment now available. The following is a list of less-common but increasingly popular fruits and vegetables showing up on menus today.

Artichoke: A vegetable with petal-shaped leaves. Artichokes are steamed and served with melted butter, mayonnaise, or other sauces. The fleshy part of the vegetable is scraped from the leaf with the teeth. Guests will need an extra plate to discard the leaves. The tender artichoke heart is also eaten.

Bok choy [bahk CHOY]: A Chinese cabbage. Bok choy tastes like a mild cabbage, but with a crisp, celery-like texture.

Broccoli rabe (raab) [RAB]: A vegetable that resembles broccoli with spinach leaves, with a biting, mustard flavor; also called rapini [rah-PEE-nee].

Celery root: A round, knobby vegetable about the size of an apple, with a nutty taste; also called celeriac [seh-LER-ee-ak].

Celery root

123

Chayote [chi-OH-tay]: A gourd with a round or pear shape and one large center seed. It has a crunchy texture and a taste similar to cucumber.

Chiles: Pungent pod-shaped vegetables that are used in cuisines all over the world. Chiles range in size, color, and shape, and also in taste, from very hot to mild. Anaheim is a long, green to red pod with a mild to hot flavor, first grown in California. Habanero [ah-bah-NEH-roh] is a short and wide, orange pod that is extremely hot in flavor. Jalapeño [hah-lah-PEH-nyoh], named after the Mexican city of Jalapa, is a blunt, green pod that has a hot flavor. Smoked and dried jalapeños are called chipotles [chih-POHT-lays]. Poblano [po-BLAH-noh] is a heart-shaped, dark green pod, with a mild to hot flavor; dried, it is called an ancho chile. Serrano [seh-RAH-noh] is a small, tubular, green pod that has a hot, acidic flavor.

Fava [FAH-vuh] **beans:** Similar to lima beans but larger and used in Middle Eastern and Mediterranean dishes.

Fennel: The fennel bulb looks like white celery with a wide, round base and feathery green leaves. It has a light licorice flavor.

Fiddlehead ferns: Bright green, tightly coiled shoots with an asparagus-like flavor and a chewy texture.

Fig: A round to oval fruit with hundreds of tiny edible seeds.

Leek: A mild, onion-like vegetable.

Mushrooms: Edible fungi. Fresh mushrooms are an important ingredient in cooking and give an earthy flavor to sauces and dishes. Chefs today use many kinds of mushrooms including button, chanterelles, cremini, enoki, morels, oyster, portobellos, porcini, shiitake, straw, and wood ears.

Nuts: A wide variety of nuts are finding their way into popular dishes. A couple of increasingly popular nuts are hazelnuts (also called filberts), which are small, round nuts that are often used in desserts; and pine nuts, which are nuts from pine trees used in many dishes, including pesto.

Olives: The small, oil-rich fruit of the olive tree, indigenous to the Mediterranean. There are dozens of varieties of olives, each with its own distinct flavor. Unripe olives are always green, but ripe olives may be green, black, or purple. Some common kinds of olives are kalamata [kahl-uh-MAH-tuh], from Greece; niçoise [nee-SWAHZ], from France; and gaeta [gah-AY-tuh], from Italy.

Olive oil: Oil produced by pressing ripe olives. Olive oil is used throughout the world for cooking and is popular for its flavor and nutritional properties. Olive oil varies in color and taste as much as wine does. Olive oils are classified according to their acidity, with extra virgin as the finest grade.

Potatoes: A popular vegetable grown around the world. The potato is a tuber, the fleshy underground stem of a plant that can grow into a new plant. In America, the potatoes varieties range in color from white to red and in texture from fluffy to waxy. Two popular varieties of potatoes in the United States are Idaho russets and Yukon gold. The yam is a large, potato-like tuber that has starchy, pale yellow flesh and is often mistaken for the sweet potato, which usually has orange flesh. Potatoes are fried, boiled, mashed, baked, sautéed, and broiled. A new potato is a small, young potato, usually boiled or steamed and served in its skin, and great for potato salads.

Salad greens: Some new, tasty greens are finding their way into restaurant salads. Arugula [ah-ROO-guh-lah] is a bitter salad green with a peppery, aromatic flavor. Endive [EN-deev] is a bitter-tasting, leafy vegetable that is similar to chicory. Frisée [free-ZAY] is a mild French endive. Radicchio [rah-DEE-kee-oh] is a lettuce-like red-leafed vegetable with a pleasantly bitter flavor.

Sorrel: An herb with leaves that look like bright green spinach. The flavor is very sour, and it is often used as a seasoning for fish, soups, and sauces.

Truffles: A fungus that flowers underground around oak or hazelnut trees. Black truffles have a nutty flavor and are used in sauces, pâtés, and foie gras. White truffles are pungent with a strong perfumy smell. They are eaten raw or are sliced thinly and served over pasta, egg dishes, and salads.

Grain Products

Bread is served at most restaurants before the meal. Bread, of course, is made from flour, which is made from grain. White bread is made from bleached flour, which is wheat flour without the bran or wheat germ. Whole-wheat bread is made from whole wheat, which includes the bran and wheat germ. Bread can also be made from rye and other grains.

Almost every country has some form of pasta, which is a combination of semolina flour (coarsely milled hard wheat flour) and water. Noodles, in contrast to pasta, are a combination of flour and egg. Rice is another type of grain that is as common as bread in many of the world's cuisines. There are literally hundreds of kinds grain products, too many for us to list, but here are some increasingly popular ones you'll encounter.

Bruschetta [broo-SHEH-tah]: An Italian bread rubbed with garlic, drenched in olive oil, salted, and served warm.

Couscous [KOOS-koos]: Granular semolina, popular in Middle Eastern cuisine.

Crêpe [CRAIP]: A thin French pancake filled with sweet or savory foods.

Crostini [kroh-STEE-nee]: Italian for "little toasts." They are similar to croutons but often used for canapés, which are hors d'oeuvres with savory toppings. Similar to croutons,

Croûte [KROOT]: The crust from a hollowed-out piece of bread, filled with savory food.

Foccaccia [foh-KAH-chyah]: A dense Italian bread, coated with olive oil and generously seasoned.

Gnocchi [NYOH-kee]: Small Italian dumplings, usually made from potato and covered with butter, cheese, or pasta sauce.

Phyllo [FEE-low] **dough:** An ultra-thin flour-based dough; used to make both savory dishes and desserts.

Pilaf [PEE-lahf] or **pilau** [pih-LOW]: Grains cooked by sautéing in butter, then simmering in stock.

Polenta [poh-LEHN-tah]: A cornmeal mush that is usually served as a side dish, hot or cold.

Risotto [ree-ZAW-toh]: A kind of rice with a high starch content; also a dish made by sautéing this kind of rice briefly in butter or oil, then cooking it in stock while stirring constantly.

Soba [SOH-buh]: Japanese noodles made from buckwheat flour.

Sourdough: A dough that contains a fermented starter instead of, or in addition to, yeast.

Dairy Products

Dairy products are foods that are made from milk. In the United States, most of this milk comes from cows.

Butter: Cream churned to a semisolid state that contains 80 percent milk fat. Drawn butter is melted butter, and clarified butter is the clear butterfat that remains when butter is slowly melted and separated, leaving the milk solids and water behind. Whipped butter is soft and light because it has air whipped into it.

Cream: The fat portion of whole milk. Light cream is the kind most commonly used for coffee, and heavy cream is used to make whipped cream and is high in milk fat. Half-and-half is half milk, half cream.

Milk: You should be aware of the different levels of milk fat in milk. Whole milk is straight from the cow and it contains about 3.5 percent fat; low-fat contains less than 2 percent fat; and nonfat, or skim, contains less than .5 percent fat.

Yogurt: Milk or milk products that have been fermented with a bacteria.

Cheese

All cheese is made from the milk of cows, goats, sheep, and sometimes other mammals. Fresh cheeses must be kept refrigerated and used quickly. These include cream cheese, ricotta cheese, and cottage cheese. Ripened cheeses are cured and aged for as long as several years. Cheese can be used as an ingredient in a dish or served alone as a separate course. In France, a selection of cheeses, served on a board or platter, is offered before the dessert course. This course is becoming increasingly popular in finer restaurants in the United States. Beyond Cheddar, Swiss, and other favorites, there are many other popular cheeses you should know.

Asiago [ah-SYAH-goh]: An aged Italian cheese made from cow's milk. It is consumed as a table cheese when six months old, or aged for a longer period of time and used for seasoning.

Feta [FEHT-uh]: The best known Greek cheese, traditionally made from goat's milk. It has a sharp, salty taste.

Gorgonzola [gohr-guhn-ZOH-lah]: An Italian cheese made from cow's milk. The blue to green colored veins in the cheese are produced by a mold. Because of the colored veins, this cheese is sometimes called a blue cheese.

Gruyère [groo-YEHR]: The most famous Swiss cheese, made from cow's milk and ripened for about a year. It has a rich, nutty flavor.

Mascarpone [mas-kahr-POH-nay]: A fresh Italian cheese made from the cream of cow's milk. It has a rich, smooth flavor and is often combined with cocoa, coffee, or other flavorings before being eaten.

Mozzarella [maht-suh-REHL-lah]: A soft, fresh Italian cheese made from cow's milk. It has a light, creamy taste.

Parmesan [PAHR-muh-zahn]: The English name for a hard Italian cheese from cow's milk. It has a tangy flavor and is often grated over pasta and other dishes.

Pecorino [peh-kuh-REE-noh]: The Italian name for any sheep's milk cheese, which can be eaten fresh or aged. Different kinds of pecorino vary widely in texture and taste.

Queso fresco [KAY-soh FRAY-skoh]: A Latin-American white cheese made from cow's milk and usually well salted; also called *queso blanco*.

Flavors and Extras

There are a number of ways to add flavor to a dish, whether by combining it into the dish (seasonings), pouring it on top (sauces), or serving it on the side (condiments). It is important for you to be able characterize these flavors and extras to guests—spicy, sweet, sour, creamy, and so on—so that they know what to expect.

Seasonings

Today's chefs use a wider diversity of seasonings than ever before, borrowing from cuisines all over the world. Each ingredient adds its own taste and fragrance to a particular dish.

Bouquet garni [boo-KAY gar-NEE]: A bundle of herbs used as a flavoring in soups, stews, and other dishes, and removed before the dish is served.

Cilantro [sih-LAHN-troh]: The pungent-flavored leaves and stems of the coriander plant.

Cocoa: The roasted, husked, and ground seeds of the cacao tree.

Ginger: The gnarled root of the ginger plant, used fresh as a seasoning or dried in a powdered form. It has a sweet, peppery flavor.

Lemongrass: A scallion-like herb used in Thai cooking to flavor dishes.

Pepper: Black pepper is ground from the dried berries, or peppercorns, of the pepper vine. White pepper is the center of the peppercorn. Its flavor is less peppery than black and is usually used in dishes that are very light in color. Since the flavor of pepper is best when the peppercorns are freshly ground, many wait persons offer to grind pepper onto a guest's food (see page 48). Different kinds of peppercorns vary in pungency, aroma, and flavor.

Rubs: A mixture of dry spices that is rubbed onto meat before cooking. Popular rub ingredients include pepper, salt, and dried garlic.

Salt: One of the most widely used condiments in the world, salt is actually sodium chloride. Different kinds of salt vary in grain size and texture. Rock salt is mined from the ground and is sometimes used for preserving foods. Sea salt is extracted from sea water and has attractive flakes or crystals. Table salt is small grained and refined for easy pouring. Kosher salt is coarsely ground, has no additives, and meets kosher standards.

Soy sauce: A dark, salty sauce that is made from fermented soybeans and that is an important ingredient in Asian cooking. Tamari is a similar sauce, but darker and thicker. Teriyaki is a marinade that combines soy sauce, sake, sugar, and other ingredients.

Vinegar: Fermented grape juice or wine used as an ingredient in cooking, marinades, and vinaigrettes. Many types of vinegar are available, each of which comes from a different source (grapes and other fruits, rice, sugar, and so on) and has a different flavor. Balsamic [bal-SAH-mihk] is a popular Italian vinegar made from white Trebbiano grape juice. It is aged like wine in barrels over a period of years.

Sauces

Chefs use sauces to enhance food by adding richness, flavor, or moisture. French cooking is famous for its sauces, and many of the sauces used by chefs today are variations on classic French sauces. In addition to French sauces, restaurant kitchens have adapted and borrowed sauces from Indian, Chinese, Mexican, and other cuisines to create new and innovative dishes.

Sauces are designed to complement a dish, either by adding a flavor that contrasts with a food or by helping to bring out the intrinsic flavor of a food. Many sauces involve the preparation of a roux, which is a mixture of flour and fat (usually butter) that cooks use to thicken a sauce or other liquid. Some sauces are made from stock, which is usually the juice of beef or some other meat. Roux and stocks are also used as bases for soups and other bowl dishes. Here are some common sauces.

Béarnaise [behr-NAYZ]: A sauce made with vinegar, wine, egg yolks, butter, and flavoring herbs, and often served with steak or flavorful grilled fish.

Béchamel [bay-shah-MEHL]: A white sauce made with a roux and milk.

Curry: A mixture of spices, including cumin, that is basic to East Indian cuisine.

Demi-glace [DEHM-ee glahs]: A sauce made from stock reduced to the consistency of light syrup.

Espagnole [ehs-pah-NYOHL]: A sauce made with stock and often used as a base for other sauces; also known as brown sauces.

Hollandaise [HOL-uhn-dayz]: A smooth, rich sauce made with butter, egg yolks, and lemon juice.

Mole [MOH-lay]: A rich, dark Mexican sauce made from garlic, chile peppers, onions, pumpkin seeds, and Mexican chocolate. Often served over meats.

Pesto [PEH-stoh]: A thick, uncooked Italian sauce made from a number of ingredients including ground basil, garlic, pine nuts, and olive oil.

Tartar: A mayonnaise-based sauce with onions or shallots.

Velouté [veh-loo-TAY]: A velvety white sauce made from a roux and veal or chicken stock.

Condiments

Condiments are herbs, sauces, and spices that are added to a dish before eating. Although some condiments are added to a meal in the kitchen, others are left on the table for guests to season their dishes to their own tastes. Beyond the standard hamburger fare (ketchup and mustard), you'll see many other condiments on today's menus.

Aïoli [ay-OH-lee]: A garlic mayonnaise.

Chutney: A sweet and spicy condiment from East India that contains fruit, vinegar, and sugar.

Crème fraîche [krehm FRESH]: A tangy French cream similar in taste and consistency to sour cream.

Fish sauce: A Southeast Asian sauce made from fermented fish.

Mayonnaise: A cold emulsified sauce made from oil beaten into egg yolks.

Salsa [SAHL-sah]: A Mexican sauce made from a variety of ingredients including tomatoes, chile peppers, and cilantro.

Tapenade [TAH-puh-nahd]: A thick French condiment made from capers, anchovies, ripe olives, olive oil, lemon juice, and seasonings.

Wasabi [WAH-sah-bee]: A green condiment similar to horseradish and often served with sushi and used in other Japanese food.

Desserts

Many restaurants craft tempting displays to show off their dessert items. Such displays are arranged on a dessert tray or cart. Make sure you know what desserts your restaurant serves. Some restaurants use dessert menus. When selling desserts, always assume that the guests will order dessert and ask them, "Would you like to see our dessert menu?" or "Should I bring out a dessert tray?" But never ask, "Did you save any room for dessert?" (See page 54 for more on serving desserts.) Here are some popular and lesser-known desserts.

Baked Alaska: A dessert with layers of ice cream, cake, and meringue.

Cake: A baked dessert with or without icing. There are two basic types of cakes: Foam cakes and butter cakes. Foam cakes include angel food cake, sponge cake, and chiffon cake. Butter cakes include pound cake, devil's food cake, and carrot cake. Sponge cake is a sweet cake made with beaten egg yolks and egg whites. Butter cakes contain fat, often in the form of butter.

Cheesecake: A cream cheese–based cake, often flavored and topped with fruit.

Cobbler: A dessert of baked fruit with a crust on the top and bottom.

Crisp: A dessert of baked fruit with a crumb topping.

Custard: A thick, creamy dessert made with eggs. Popular custards include crème brûlée [krehm broo-LAY] and flan [FLAHN].

Galette [GAH-leht]: A round, flat cake or tart.

Gelato [jeh-LAH-toh]: A rich, dense Italian ice cream.

Marzipan: A paste of sugar, ground almonds, and egg whites, used to make candies and in cakes.

Meringue [muh-RANG]: Egg whites beaten until stiff, then sweetened.

Mousse [MOOSE]: A French word for "foam," used to describe a dish with a foamy texture, made from beaten egg whites or whipped cream folded into a mixture. Chocolate mousse is a favorite cold dessert, but some types of mousse are savory and served hot.

Napoleon: A glazed pastry made from layers of puff pastry and pastry cream; also used to refer to layered savory dishes.

Pie: A dessert made with a crust in a shallow, round pan. Pies can be filled with a variety of ingredients including fruit, whipped cream, or custard. There are also savory pies, which can be filled with chicken, beef, vegetables, and other ingredients.

Pudding: A creamy dessert thickened with cornstarch or flour. Popular puddings include rice pudding and bread pudding.

Sauces: Dessert sauces add extra sweetness, fruitiness, moisture, or taste contrasts to a dessert. Popular dessert sauces include caramel sauce, chocolate sauce, and fruit sauce. A sabayon [sah-bah-YAWN] is a dessert sauce made with wine, a coulis [koo-LEE] is a puréed fruit sauce, and crème anglaise [krehm-ahn-GLEHZ] is a popular rich custard sauce.

Sherbet: A frozen fruit-flavored dessert, sometimes made with milk or egg whites.

Sorbet [sor-BAY]: A frozen fruit-flavored dessert, similar to sherbet.

Soufflé [soo-FLAY]: A light and fluffy dessert made from a flavored base, such as chocolate or lemon, folded with beaten egg whites and baked. Soufflés are often ordered before a meal, as they are difficult to make, and many restaurants prepare them per order.

Tart: A baked dish similar to a pie, comprised of a filled pastry crust with no top crust. Tarts can also be filled with fruit, custard, or other sweet or savory foods.

Torte: A rich, multilayered butter cake, not to be confused witha *tart*.

Preparation terms

Now that you are familiar with basic foods, it is important for you to understand how the chef prepares them. Read through the following list of terms, and when you see a cooking method used to describe a dish on the menu, make sure you know what it means. *Pan-seared tuna, blackened redfish,* and *roasted peppers* are a few examples of how cooking methods are used in menu descriptions. There are also terms that describe the style in which a food is prepared, such as *tomato aspic, lobster bisque,* or *mushroom pâté.* Here's what some of those descriptions mean.

À la mode [ah lah MODE]: A French term meaning "in the style of," used to describe alternate preparations of a single dish. In the United States, it generally refers to a serving of pie topped with ice cream.

Al dente [al DEN-tay]: Pasta that is cooked through but very slightly chewy; the Italian phrase means "to the tooth."

Aspic: A clear jelly made from stock or juices and mixed with gelatin. It is used primarily as a garnish.

Baked: Cooked in an oven.

Barbecued: Slow cooked at a low temperature in an enclosed grill or smoker using the hot smoke of a wood fire.

Basted: Moistened by pouring liquids onto a food while cooking.

Batter: A mixture of liquid, flour, and other ingredients; used in making pancakes, cakes, and other baked or fried foods.

Bisque: A rich, creamy soup made from a vegetable or crustacean purée.

Blackened: Seasoned and cooked over high heat in a heavy skillet until charred.

"The key to everything is to enjoy yourself. Eating is the one great sensual pleasure that we all enjoy several times a day. So go ahead and have fun with the entire process of obtaining foodstuffs, preparing and cooking them, and serving them forth."

—CHARLIE TROTTER, *The Kitchen Sessions*

Blanched: Briefly cooked in boiling water.

Boiled: Cooked by immersion in a boiling liquid.

Bouillabaisse [BOO-yah-baze]: A seafood stew from the south of France.

Bouillon [boo-YAWN]: The French term for "broth."

Braised: Cooked slowly in a small amount of liquid at low heat for a long time in a tightly covered pan. Sometimes the food is browned first. This method is used for less-tender cuts of meat.

Brine: A salty solution used to preserve foods like pickles, and to add moisture to foods that will be cooked, such as turkey, chicken, and pork chops.

Broiled: Cooked directly under a heat source.

Broth: A savory liquid made by simmering spices, vegetables, herbs, or meat in water or stock.

Butterfly: To cut a food such as shrimp so that the two halves of the food open out like a butterfly.

Canapé [can-a-PAY]: An hors d'oeuvre made from a small piece of bread or toast topped with a savory item.

Caramelized: Coated with sugar and cooked until brown; or foods that naturally contain sugar and are cooked until brown, such as onion.

Carved: Sliced, referring to meats, fish, and other foods. This is usually done at the table by the wait person.

Casserole: A French word referring to a dish cooked in a heavy container that usually has two handles and a lid. The word also refers to the container itself.

Chop: A small cut of meat that usually includes part of the rib. Also, to cut up a food into small, equal pieces.

Chowder: A thick stew or soup.

Confit [con-FEE]: Meat, such as duck, cooked and served in its own fat, usually served cold.

Consommé [con-so-MAY]: A strong, clear broth from which the impurities have been removed.

Crudités [krew-dee-TAY]: Small pieces of raw vegetables served with a dip.

Cured: Preserved by salting, drying, or smoking (usually meat or fish).

Deep-fried: Cooked by immersing a food in hot fat.

Deglaze: To add liquid to a pan in which food has been cooked and then stir to scrape up the browned bits from the bottom of the pan.

Deviled: Mixed with hot sauce, mustard, or other spicy seasonings.

Diced: Cut into small cubes of equal size.

Dressed: A food item that has been prepared for cooking.

Dumpling: A small piece of dough or batter item that is steamed, simmered, or poached and sometimes filled with sweet or savory foods.

Egg wash: Beaten egg combined with a liquid to brush over foods that will be baked to make them shine.

Emulsion: A combination of liquids, one oil- or fat-based and one water-based.

Essence: The concentrated flavor extracted from a food such as vanilla beans.

Étouffée [ay-too-FAY]: A Cajun stew of crayfish and vegetables.

Filé [FEE-lay]: A sauce thickener made from ground sassafras and often used in gumbo.

Fillet [fih-LAY]: A boneless piece of fish, cut lengthwise from end to end.

Fricassee [frick-a-SEE]: A stew of meat such as poultry.

Fried: Cooked in a skillet with a small amount of oil or fat; also called *panfried.*

Fritter: A food that is made with batter, or a deep-fried, battered food.

Garni [gar-NEE]: The French word for "garnish," an edible decoration added to a food before serving.

Glazed: Brushed with a sauce for a shiny coating.

Gratin [gra-TAN]: A browned crust on the top of a dish, usually made with cheese or crumbs.

Griddle: A heavy metal surface on which foods such as pancakes are cooked directly.

Grilled: Cooked on a grill over hot coals, wood, or gas.

Gumbo: A Cajun soup or stew made with filé and okra.

Hash: A mixture of chopped meat and vegetables that is panfried.

Hors d'oeuvre [or DERVE]: An appetizer, usually a small finger food.

Infusion: A combination of a liquid and one or more flavoring agents that are steeped to extract the flavor.

Julienned [zhoo-LYEND]: Food cut into $^1/_8$-inch-thick strips.

Jus [ZHOO]: The French term for juice. Refers to the liquid naturally exuded from cooked foods.

Marinade: A liquid used to flavor or tenderize food. The food is usually soaked in marinade for a time before cooking. Also refers to the soaking process itself.

Medallion: A small, round cut of meat.

Minced: Chopped into tiny pieces.

Nouvelle cuisine [noo-VELL quee-ZEEN]: The French term for "new cooking." A type of cooking that emphasizes fresh, light ingredients.

Paella [pie-AY-uh]: A Spanish dish made from rice cooked with shellfish, meat, and vegetables.

Pan gravy: A gravy or sauce made from pan drippings combined with a roux or other ingredients.

Panbroiled: Cooked by broiling in a hot pan with little fat.

Panfried: Cooked in a skillet in a small amount of oil or fat.

Parcooked: Cooked partially; similar to blanching, though blanching is usually briefer.

Paring knife: A knife with a short blade used for trimming vegetables and meats.

Pâté [pah-TAY]: A savory mixture of chopped ground meat, fish, or vegetables, with spices and other ingredients.

Poached: Cooked gently in liquid.

Puréed [pew-RAID]: Finely blended to a smooth consistency in a blender or food processor.

Ragoût [ra-GOO]: A stew or meaty tomato sauce.

Reduced: Thickened or concentrated by boiling so that some of the liquid is evaporated and the flavor is enhanced.

Rendered: Cooked until a food releases its fat.

Roasted: Dry-cooked in a uncovered shallow pan in an oven or over a fire.

Round: A cut of beef from the generally tough hindquarters, which include the rump, sirloin tip, and eye of round, and the tenderer top and bottom rounds.

Roux: A cooked mixture of flour and butter or oil, used to thicken soups or sauces.

Sashimi [sah-SHEE-mee]: A Japanese dish of sliced raw fish served with diakon radish, gingerroot, wasabi, and soy sauce.

Sautéed: Cooked quickly in a small amount of oil or fat in a skillet or sauté pan over direct heat.

Savory: A food or dish that is not sweet.

Scalded: Heated to just below the boiling point.

Scored: Cut on the surface at even intervals so that the food cooks through.

Seared: Browned quickly over very high heat, either in a skillet, under a broiler, or in an oven.

Shirred egg: An egg cooked in butter in a small dish under a broiler.

Simmer: To cook in a liquid that is just below the boiling point.

Skim: To remove foam or fat from the surface of a liquid.

Smoked: Foods that have been flavored or cooked by exposure to aromatic smoke from certain woods.

Smorgasbord: A Scandinavian buffet of cold foods.

Soufflé [soo-FLAY]: A dish prepared with beaten egg whites that puffs up while cooking.

Steamed: Cooked over, but not in, a boiling liquid in a covered pan.

Stewed: Food cooked as small pieces in a liquid; also refers to the dish itself.

Stir-fried: Chopped into small pieces and quickly fried with a little hot oil in a Chinese pan known as a *wok*.

Stock: An intensely flavored liquid made from simmered vegetables and meat, poultry, or fish. Used as a base for soups and sauces.

Stone-ground: Flour or other meal that has been milled between stones.

Sushi [SOO-shee]: A Japanese specialty, based on flavored boiled rice made into rolls with other ingredients such as chopped vegetables, and raw fish.

Sweat: To cook vegetables or other food in a covered pan with a small amount of fat until the food softens.

Temper: To heat gradually and gently, as in beating a cooked mixture into beaten eggs when making custard. Chocolate is tempered, or heated to a certain point, to produce a shiny chocolate that will not turn gray.

Tempura: A Japanese dish of vegetables or shrimp that are coated in a light batter and deep-fried.

Trussed: Tied with a string prior to cooking to achieve a compact shape (usually poultry or meat).

Tureen: A large container with a ladle, usually for serving soup.

Whipped: Beaten rapidly so to incorporate air and become frothy, as with egg whites or cream.

Wok: A round-bottomed cooking utensil used to panfry foods over high heat.

ON YOUR OWN

The best way to learn about food is to sample all kinds of dishes and cuisines. Try French, Italian, German, Greek, Spanish, Mexican, Chinese, Japanese, and Thai food. Experiment and learn to enjoy the adventure of discovering new tastes. Read cookbooks, watch cooking shows, cook for friends, and go out to good restaurants. *Good* does not necessarily mean expensive. Pay attention to the produce and meat counters at your grocery store. Find a really good market and spend an afternoon browsing the counters and aisles. Good food is one of the great joys of life. And if you are in the restaurant business, knowing food will make you more successful and boost your income.

CHAPTER 9

SANITATION, SAFETY, AND LIABILITY

When guests come into your restaurant, you should strive to provide them with a memorable dining experience. And although it's not always mentioned, you must also provide them with a safe dining experience.

Issues of sanitation or cleanliness, safe food-handling practices, and customer safety are very important. Not only can failures in these areas ruin your guests' evening, they can also make them sick. Sometimes, guests have even died because of improper restaurant sanitation. And when guests are sickened or injured, problems of liability can occur. *Liability* means being legally bound to compensate individuals for injuries. Both restaurant owners and employees may be liable for injuries suffered by guests.

Most states, counties, and cities have regulations dealing with the training and certification of food handlers. These training classes tend to be rather technical, but the issues are very important.

Sanitation

Personal hygiene is very important. Your whole body should be clean before you come to work. You need to look (and smell) like the professional that you are.

When waiting tables, your hands come in contact with food, dirty dishes, money, and many unsanitary items. Many of these objects carry germs and bacteria that can cause health problems.

It is vitally important that you keep your hands clean and wash them often during your shift. To properly sanitize your hands, you must wash them for 20 seconds with soap or a soap substitute in warm water.

Wash your hands for 20 seconds.

You should never touch your hair, face, or body after you properly wash your hands. While you never want to touch a guest's food, there will be times when you are in contact with the food and will have an opportunity to transmit germs. Be very aware of your hands and make sure they're always clean.

ON YOUR OWN

Wash your hands long enough to sanitize them. Sing "Happy Birthday" to yourself while washing your hands; that song is about 20 seconds long.

Injuries and Illness

We all know the importance of not coming in contact with blood or body fluids. It is important that any open sore or cut be properly treated and bandaged. Never touch any food or beverage if you have a cut or sore and do not have it bandaged properly. You run the risk of spreading an infection, and you could also cause your wound to become infected and not heal properly. Make sure that any bandage is secured so that there is no chance that it may fall off into someone's food.

If you have a cold, the flu, or some other sickness, you should not be handling food. Your manager may be able to use you in a another capacity. Inform your manager of your illness and follow the restaurant's policy for handling employee illnesses.

Be aware of germs and bacteria and how you may be transmitting them. Never cough, sneeze, or breathe on anyone's food. This is a very serious issue, as a case of food poisoning or an outbreak of an illness can ruin a business. More important than that, the restaurant industry owes guests a safe and enjoyable experience.

Germs and Unsanitary Practices

Germs can kill, or at least make people so ill they wish they were dead. Most people can handle a few germs in their food and not become ill. Children, the elderly, and people with any immune deficiency, however, are very susceptible to illnesses caused by germs and viruses. Make sure that any produce that you serve is rinsed, including the lemons for iced tea.

Never chew gum while working in a restaurant. Besides being unsightly, chewing gum can spread disease. When you chew, you spit, and the saliva you spit can spread bacteria to the food you are serving.

You must also avoid eating around food that is being prepared for guests. Don't sample foods in the kitchen, never stick your fingers into any food that is being served, and never eat off a guest's plate (no matter how tempting the french fries look).

Be aware of how food-borne illnesses are spread, know safe food-handling practices, and report any violations or unsafe practices to management. Also, be sure to keep cleaning chemicals away from food.

Food-Borne Illnesses and Cross-Contamination

Food poisoning is not just an upset stomach; it is a serious and painful illness caused by eating spoiled or contaminated food. It can lead to hospitalization and even death in some cases.

Food poisoning is most often caused by unsafe food-handling and food-storage practices or by cross-contamination. *Cross-contamination* means transferring germs from one item to another. Examples of cross-contamination include blood or scraps from a raw food product coming in contact with a prepared food product, or a cleaning fluid coming into contact with a food.

Whenever a food is prepared, or *prepped,* the area must be sanitized before another food is prepared. The hands of the preparer must also be sanitized. Raw foods and cooked foods should never come in contact with one another. Any cleaning supplies must be kept away from exposed foods.

Food must be stored using the FIFO method to ensure freshness. *FIFO* stands for "first in, first out," which means that the foods that go into a storage area first should also be brought out first. Food must be stored at the proper temperatures. Foods needing refrigeration or freezing must be put away promptly to ensure their freshness. Food must also be cooked properly and thoroughly. Cooked food must be stored at proper temperatures. The danger zone at which bacteria will grow in cooked food is between 41° and 140°F. Food must not be held or stored within this temperature zone.

Most of the issues of food handling and storage are the responsibility of the kitchen manager and the cooks. However, safe food handling and illness prevention are crucial areas of concern for the restaurant industry, and all restaurant employees should be trained in safe food handling and be aware of any possible food-safety violations.

One recent discovery is that iced tea can be a source of food-related illness. Because tea leaves are organic, bacteria can grow on them. Most tea brewers do not heat the tea to a point where all bacteria is killed. Therefore, it is important to keep tea urns clean and sanitized. Never save any leftover iced tea to use on another shift.

Safety

Keep on the lookout for any unsafe situations. Managers are responsible for making sure that the building is maintained, that the building and parking areas are safe, and that any emergency equipment such as fire extinguishers are available. You can do your part by watching for unsafe situations and acting quickly to fix them.

- Did someone spill water on the floor? Wipe it up immediately.
- Did someone spill a large tray of food on the floor? Warn coworkers and guests and make sure the area is cleaned up as soon as possible.
- Is a section of the restaurant dark because the lightbulbs have burned out? Report it to the manager.
- Is there a broken chair? Tell the manager so he or she can replace it.

Preventing Accidents

The most effective way to minimize accidents and injuries on the job is, of course, to take precautions to make sure they don't happen. This means you need to be responsible and alert while performing all of your tasks in both the front and the back of the house.

- Be sure that you are properly trained on any kitchen equipment you might be near, especially slicers.
- Be careful when carrying something. Alert those around you when carrying hot items, especially around a corner. "Hot," or "Coming around, hot," are common restaurant phrases used to warn others of danger.
- Be careful of swinging doors. Always use the door on the right side to avoid collisions.
- Pay attention to what you are doing when you have a sharp instrument in your hand.

Above all, don't be careless. Always be aware of the risks in your job and perform it safely. Most injuries are preventable. Don't cause accidents by being careless.

Despite even the best precautions, someone in your restaurant may be seriously injured. Make sure that you know the location of first-aid supplies. Many states require that restaurants post information on performing first aid. Someone on duty should be certified in performing cardiopulmonary resuscitation, or CPR. Every employee should know how to perform the Heimlich maneuver on choking victims.

Liability

Broken dishes. Cut fingers. Dropped trays. Burns. Accidents are bound to happen. When they do, it's your duty to make the comfort and safety of your guests your first concern, and then clean up the mess. Hopefully, your coworkers and management will quickly come to your aid. If another wait person has an accident, help him or her out as well. You are all on the same team.

Handle accidents as quickly and discreetly as possible. Sometimes the guests will need to be relocated to another table. In some cases, another wait person should take over the table if the first wait person is injured or attending to an injured guest. Inform your floor manager of the situation as soon as possible.

For small spills on clothing, club soda is often helpful in preventing the stain from setting. Bring a small glass of club soda and a napkin to the table for the guest to use to clean the stain. It is customary for the restaurant to offer to pay for the cleaning bill of any soiled clothing.

Accidents will happen.

146

Everyone knows that accidents happen. But these days, your restaurant and its employees may be held liable for any injuries you cause your guests. This means that you might have to pay money to any guests that you injure while on the job.

Handling Sick Guests

Guests sometimes become ill in the restaurant, whether from something they've eaten, from simply eating too much rich food, or from some other cause altogether. No matter what the reason for a guest's distress, show immediate, genuine concern for his or her condition. If the person wishes to lie down, find a place in an office or another part of the restaurant.

Once you have made sure that the person is as comfortable as possible, get all the relevant information: name, address and phone number, what the person ate and drank, and whether or not anyone else in the party is ill.

Never say anything that implies that you or the restaurant accept blame for the illness, but be very concerned. Offer to reimburse the guest for the meal or send a gift certificate. If medical attention is needed, the guest may be reimbursed for any expenses, depending on restaurant policy. Alert the kitchen to check any items that may have caused the sickness. Check for safe food-handling practices in the kitchen as well. If you think you have a problem, talk to your manager. Perhaps it will be advisable to call your local health department for aid in fixing the problem or retraining.

Follow the same procedure if you get a call from a guest who ate at your restaurant and later fell sick. Again, show immediate concern, get all the relevant information, and offer to reimburse the person for the meal in question or send a gift certificate. A cooperative guest who became ill because of a mistake on the part of your restaurant can provide valuable help in making sure that no one else encounters the same situation.

Legal Issues

The laws concerning sanitation, safety, and liability vary from state to state and even county to county. In Texas, front-of-the-house staff are required to take a three-hour course in sanitation and food safety. Some counties in Texas demand TB tests, chest X-rays, and physicals. Other counties require only safe food-handling training. Some require a combination of both a physical exam and training. Others require all employees to be certified in sanitation, while some require that only managers be certified.

Make sure you know the legal requirements regarding sanitation and safety training in your state and county. In these times of heightened security, customers are more aware than ever of the necessity for safe food handling. For more information, contact your state or city restaurant association, or call the National Restaurant Association at 202-331-5900.

Businesses owe their guests a safe and enjoyable experience and must be prepared to prevent and to react to any situations that affect their safety and well-being. Management should train its employees on how to handle all emergencies, from robberies to fires. Know the location of fire exits and the evacuation plan for your restaurant. It may save a guest's life—and your own.

CHAPTER 10

FINANCES AND TIPS

The restaurant industry is highly competitive. The profit margin is very low. All restaurant employees—especially wait staff—should be knowledgeable about the restaurant business and do their part to increase sales and to control expenses.

In most retail businesses, the business owners buy finished products and sell them directly to customers. The restaurant business is different. Restaurants buy raw food products that are stored, prepared, and sold. A restaurant is actually a factory, a storage facility, and a retail business all in one.

Because so much goes on in a restaurant, the actions of all the employees can affect the bottom line. Waste, spoilage, and *pilferage,* or theft, can have a huge impact on the financial health of any restaurant. If you like your job, help your managers and owners stay in business. A successful business is a profitable business for everyone involved.

How Money Is Made

Most restaurants determine how much profit they have made by first figuring the price of the food and beverages purchased, divided by the amount of food sales. This equals the food and beverage costs, which are expressed in percentages. For example:

$$\frac{\$30,000 \text{ food purchases}}{\$100,000 \text{ food sales}} = 30 \text{ percent food costs}$$

Along with the outlay of funds for food and beverages, the staff has to be paid as well. Staff costs are referred to as *payroll*, or *labor costs*. Food costs plus payroll costs are referred to as *prime costs*.

After the prime costs are paid, the restaurant has many other expenses to pay, including rent, taxes, utilities, insurance, linen costs, advertising, pest control, cleaning, maintenance, office supplies, kitchen equipment, dishes, glasses, and silverware. What is left from sales after the prime costs and associated expenses are paid is the *profit*, which is also referred as the *bottom line*. The average restaurant in the United States makes a profit of 4 percent. An easy way to relate to the profit is to think that for every dollar the restaurant makes in sales, it keeps about 4 cents. That is not a lot of money. The small rate of profits for a restaurant is the reason that owners and managers are constantly monitoring sales, costs, and waste.

The wait staff helps a restaurant to make a profit in two ways: by helping control costs and by increasing sales. Wait persons help control costs by:

- Cutting down on waste by properly storing food items using the FIFO ("first in, first out") method
- Cutting down on linen costs by mopping up spills with rags instead of napkins
- Accurately communicating with the bar and the kitchen to minimize waste

- Serving the proper amounts of bread, butter, cream, and condiments
- Avoiding careless disposal of silverware and dishes
- Cutting down on the breakage of dishes and glasses by carrying them correctly

You can help increase revenue by:

- Making every sale possible
- Properly charging for all the food and beverage items sold
- Collecting the full amount for every item sold

Some people believe that because they work in a restaurant, they should be able to eat there too. This makes as much sense as thinking that if you work in a jewelry store, you deserve a diamond ring. Some restaurants have employee meal policies. Most restaurants forbid their staff to eat at all during their shift. Ask your manager about your restaurant's meal policy and follow it. No matter what policy your restaurant has, don't come to work hungry. When you arrive at the restaurant, you should be ready to work, not eat, unless your restaurant offers pre-shift meals.

Pilferage is another problem that affects the bottom line. Most restaurant employees who engage in pilferage don't think of it as stealing, but that's exactly what it is. Don't think you can outwit a restaurant manager. No matter what scheme you think up, someone else has tried it before you. Some of the most common forms of pilferage include:

- Taking home condiments
- Taking steaks and other foods at closing time
- Stealing silverware

Remember, pilferage is theft. If you are caught, you won't just lose your job—you could go to jail.

Paying the House

Most computerized *point-of-sale (POS) systems* process the payment of your employee checks and balance out how much you owe the house or how much the house owes you. Be careful to check the POS system report carefully.

Tipping Out

Some restaurants require that the wait staff *tip out,* that is, share their tips with a coworker—a bartender or a bus person, for example. Different restaurants use different systems to tip out. Some use a percentage of sales, others use a percentage of your tips. On average, about 25 percent of wait staff tips are tipped out.

Make sure you understand clearly the tip-out system at your restaurant. It is your responsibility to make sure everyone in your restaurant gets the tips they deserve.

Reporting Tip Income and Record Keeping

Most wait staff are paid the minimum wage for tipped employees, which is lower than the minimum wage for nontipped employees.

You pay income taxes based on your hourly wages plus tips reported. The law states that you must report 100 percent of your tips.

The Internal Revenue Service (IRS) has been cracking down on under-reporting tips by aggressively auditing restaurants and tipped employees. It is your responsibility as a taxpayer to maintain accurate records and to be able to prove to the IRS that you have reported all of your income. Accurate income records for waiting should include the following information: amount of cash sales, amount of charge sales, amount of cash tips, amount of charge tips, and total tips earned daily. Keep your income records for at least seven years after the income has been reported to the IRS.

If you are required to tip out, you must record the name of the person you tipped and how much you tipped them. The balance is your net tips earned. You must report this amount to the restaurant in the form of a *tip report*. You must also report it to the IRS. Make sure that your records are accurate. You will need them in case you are audited by the IRS or your state revenue agency.

The IRS has done a good job of publishing clear information about the rules and regulations regarding tip income. Below, we have listed some of the most common questions about tipping and the answers as given by the IRS in their guide for employees *Tips on Tips*.

✳ TIPS ON TIPS ✳

Is my tip income taxable income?

As an employee of a food and beverage establishment, the tip income you receive—whether cash or included in a charge—is taxable income. As income, these tips are subject to federal income tax, Social Security, and Medicare taxes, and may be subject to state income tax as well.

Is there a difference between cash tips and credit card tips?

For purposes of reporting to the IRS, there is no difference between cash tips and credit card tips. Both kinds of tip income have to be recorded and reported as taxable income.

Do I have to report all my tips to my boss?

If you received $20 or more in tips in any one month, you should report all your tips to your employer so that federal income tax, Social Security, and Medicare taxes, and maybe state income tax can be withheld.

Do I have to report all my tips on my tax return?

Yes. All tips are income and should be reported on your tax return.

I was told that I had to report only 8 percent of my total sales as tips. Is this true?

No. You must report to your employer all (100 percent) tips you receive, except for the tips from any month that do not total at least $20. The 8 percent allocation rule is a requirement placed on the employer.

Here's how the 8 percent rule works: The employer has to determine if the employees have reported tips in the aggregate of at least 8 percent of the establishment's gross sales subject to tipping. To put it another way, the employer adds all the establishment's gross receipts (sales where tipping is involved). Then the employer figures 8 percent of that number. If all the employees' reported tips total less than that 8 percent figure, the employer figures out the difference between what the employees reported and the 8 percent amount. The employer then allocates that difference.

Sometimes I don't get tips directly from customers, but rather from another employee. Do I need to report those tips?

Yes. Employees who receive tips from another employee are required to report "tip-outs." Employees often disburse tips out of their earned tips to another employee (tip-outs). Remember, all tips are taxable income.

Do I have to report tip-outs that I pay to other employees?

No. You report to your employer only the amount of tips you retain. However, you must maintain records of tip-outs with your other tip income (cash tips, charged tips, split tips, tip pool).

What type of records do I have to keep?

You must keep a running daily log of all your tip income. You can use Publication 1244, Employee's Daily Record of Tips and Report to Employer, to record your tip income for one year. Publication 1244 includes Form 4070, Employee's Report of Tips to Employer, and Form 4070A, Employee's Daily Record of Tips. These forms have spacing for you to log your name, the employer's name and address, the date tips were received, the date of entry, tips received, tips paid out, and the name of the employee paid. Your daily log would be your best proof should your income tax return be questioned. You can receive copies of Publication 1244 and Form 4070 by calling 1-800-829-3676, toll free.

What can happen if I do not keep a record of my tips?

If it is determined in an examination that you underreported your tip income, the IRS will assess the taxes you owe based on the best available records of your employer. Tip income adds up. Underreporting could result in your owing substantial taxes, penalties, and interest.

If I report all my tips to my employer, do I still have to keep records?

Yes. You should keep a daily log of your tips so that in case of an examination, you can substantiate the actual amount of tips received. There are a number of reasons why you might need records:

1. Your return could be randomly selected for a federal income tax examination. For example: Your Form 1040, U.S. Individual Income Tax Return, establishes that you have your own home, two cars, and three exemptions, and your Form W-2 shows that you earned only $10,000 in income. In this scenario, an examination may occur if the examiner determines that income may have been underreported.

2. A tip examiner could review your employer's books and records. The examination could reveal unreported tip income that you may later need to verify.

3. An Internal Revenue Service Center may run a match of your income information from your Form 1040, *U.S. Individual Income Tax Return,* with the income information from your Form W-2. If these figures do not match, you could receive a notice about the discrepancy and a possible examination of your tax return.

I forgot to report my tip income to my employer, but I remembered to report it on my federal income tax return. Will that present a problem?

If you don't report your tip income to your employer, but you do report the tip income on your federal income tax return, you may owe a 50 percent Social Security and Medicare tax penalty and be subject to a negligence penalty and possibly an estimated-tax penalty. When you don't report your tips to your employer, it places your employer at risk of possible assessment of the employer's share of Social Security and Medicare taxes.

If I report all my tips, but my taxes on the tips are greater than my pay from my employer, how do I pay the remaining taxes?

You can either pay the tax when you file your federal income tax return or you can reach into your tip money and give some to your employer to be applied to those under-withheld taxes. The employer will then record these taxes and you will get credit on your Form W-2. If you wait to pay when you file your tax return, you may be subject to an estimated-tax penalty.

What can happen if I don't report my tips to the IRS?

If the IRS determines through an examination that you underreported your tips, you could be subject to additional federal income tax, Social Security and Medicare taxes, and maybe state income tax. Also, a penalty of 50 percent of the additional Social Security and Medicare taxes, and a negligence penalty of 20 percent of the additional income tax, plus interest, may apply.

What's in it for me if I report all my tip income?

There are many good reasons why you want to report all your tip income:

1. Increased income may improve financing approval when applying for mortgage, car, and other loans.
2. Increased workers' compensation benefits, should you get hurt on the job.
3. Increased unemployment compensation benefits.
4. Increased Social Security and Medicare benefits (the more you pay, the greater your benefits).
5. Increased employee pension, annuity, or 401(k) participation.
6. Check with your employer for other increased benefits (based on pay) your restaurant may offer, such as life insurance, disability, and the right to purchase stock options.
7. Compliance with the tax law.

My employer has entered into a compliance agreement with the IRS concerning tips. What is this?

The national Tip Rate Determination/Education Program was developed in 1993 to help those employees receiving tip income and their employers understand the laws on reporting tip income. Under this program, the employer can enter into one of two arrangements—the Tip Rate Determination Agreement (TRDA) or the Tip Reporting Alternative Commitment (TRAC) (created in June 1995). You can ask your employer for more information about this program.

What is my responsibility, as an employee, under the Tip Rate Determination Agreement?

You are required to file your federal tax returns. You must sign a Tipped Employee Participation Agreement proclaiming that you are participating in the program. The employer, as a participant in the TRDA, has agreed with the IRS to a tip rate for the employer's establishment. To stay a participating employee, you must report tips at or above the tip rate determined by the agreement. Further, as part of the TRDA arrangement, the employer is required to report your name, Social Security number, the hours worked or sales made, your job classification, and your reported tips to the IRS if you do not report tips at or above the determined tip rate.

What is my responsibility, as an employee, under the Tip Reporting Alternative Commitment?

Directly tipped employee:
  1. Your employer will furnish you a written statement (at least monthly) reflecting your charged tips.
  2. You are to verify or correct this statement.
  3. You are to indicate the amount of cash tips received.
  4. When reporting your cash tips, you should remember that there is a correlation between charged tips and cash tips. (Your employer may be able to inform you of the establishment's charged-sales-to-cash-sales ratio. For example, if the establishment is 50 percent charge and 50 percent cash, and you received and reported $100 in tips on charged receipts, it is reasonable to believe that you should be reporting close to $100 in cash tips.)
  5. You may be asked to provide the name and amount of any tip-outs to indirectly tipped employees.

Indirectly tipped employee:
  1. You are required to report all your tips to your employer. If the establishment has the directly tipped employee provide the name and amount of tips shared with you, the establishment could provide you with a statement of tips that you would need to verify or correct.

Does tip income reporting apply only to employees in the food and beverage industry?

No. Anyone who receives tip income is required by law to report it to his or her employer. The Tip Rate Determination/ Education Program (TRD/EP) was first promoted in the gaming (casino) industry in Las Vegas, Nevada, and subsequently spread to the food and beverage industry. Other individuals who receive tip income include airport skycaps, bartenders, hair stylists, bellhops, casino workers, delivery service people, hotel housekeepers, manicurists, masseuses, parking attendants, railroad redcaps, and taxi drivers.

Why should I report my tips to my employer?

When you report your tip income to your employer, the employer is required to withhold federal income taxes, Social Security and Medicare taxes, and maybe state income tax. Tip reporting may increase your Social Security credits, resulting in greater Social Security and Medicare benefits when you retire. Tip reporting may also increase other benefits to which you may become entitled, such as unemployment benefits, workers' compensation, or retirement benefits. Additionally, a larger income may improve financing approval for mortgage, car, and other loans.

Why has tip reporting become such an issue?

To report all tip income has always been the law. The IRS has put greater emphasis on reporting tip income over the past few years because a significant number of taxpayers are not reporting all tip earnings as income.

How can I get more information?

The IRS provides the following publications and forms relating to tip income reporting. These materials can be downloaded from the IRS Web site at www.irs.ustreas.gov and ordered through the IRS by calling 1-800-829-3676. You can also get IRS forms with instructions faxed back to you when you dial 703-368–9694 on a fax machine and follow the voice prompts.

Pub 505: *Tax Withholding and Estimated Tax.*
Pub 531: *Reporting Tip Income.*
Pub 1244: *Employee's Daily Record of Tips and Report to Employers.*
  This publication includes Form 4070, *Employee's Report of Tips to Employer,* and Form 4070A, *Employee's Daily Record of Tips.*
Form 1040ES: *Estimated Tax for Individuals.*
Form 4137: *Social Security and Medicare Tax on Unreported Tip Income.*

FiNDiNG (AND kEEPiNG) youR JoB

As a wait person, you also are a salesperson. You must take that same approach during the interview process. You must sell yourself.

The first step is to choose a restaurant where you think you might like to work. Visit various restaurants in your neighborhood. Do you like the atmosphere? Does the restaurant seem to be crowded? Do you like the service? If so, you would probably like to work at that restaurant.

Once you have chosen a restaurant, go to the restaurant and ask to fill out a job application. Restaurant managers and chefs spend a great amount of time and money making sure their dining rooms and plate presentations are as pleasing to their guests as possible. They must show great attention to detail. You should show the same attention to detail when you go to a restaurant to fill out an application. First impressions are very important. Women should wear appropriate business attire. Men should wear dress pants, a pressed shirt, and a tie. Make sure that your shoes are shined, your nails are

159

clean, and your hair is washed. Pay attention to the details of your personal grooming. Sell yourself through your first impression.

Filling Out the Application

When you go to a restaurant to ask for a job application, pick a time when the restaurant is not busy. It does not make a good first impression to walk in at noon during a busy lunch and ask to see the manager for a job application. Call the restaurant and ask for the best time to come by and fill out an application.

Usually, the best times to apply for a job at a restaurant are just as it opens for business, or during the midafternoon, between the lunch and dinner rushes. Be prepared to fill out the application when you arrive at the restaurant. You will need the following:

- A list of your previous work experience, with dates, employers, and reasons for leaving jobs. Be careful how you word these reasons. We have actually seen an application where the reason for leaving was "the manager was a jerk." This is not an appropriate response to the question. Negative comments do not give a good impression. Be honest, but be tactful.
- Names, addresses, and telephone numbers of three references. *References* are people who have known you for over a year who are not related to you.
- Your own pen.

When filling out the application, write legibly. Answer every question, and make sure that your responses are honest. Falsifying a job application is grounds for dismissal in most cases.

If you have not had any experience as a wait person, list the training that you have done, including your study of this book. In fact, bring this book along and show it to your interviewer. It could be a way to break the ice and give you a chance to demonstrate what you know about the waiting game even if you have had no previous experience.

APPLICATION FOR EMPLOYMENT
PRE-EMPLOYMENT QUESTIONNAIRE
EQUAL OPPORTUNITY EMPLOYER

Personal Information
DATE:

NAME (LAST NAME FIRST)		SOCIAL SECURITY NUMBER	
PRESENT ADDRESS	CITY	STATE	ZIP CODE
PERMANENT ADDRESS	CITY	STATE	ZIP CODE
PHONE NUMBER ( )	REFERRED BY		

Employment Desired

POSITION	DATE YOU CAN START	SALARY DESIRED
ARE YOU EMPLOYED? ☐ YES ☐ NO	IF SO, MAY WE INQUIRE OF YOUR PRESENT EMPLOYER? ☐ YES ☐ NO	
EVER APPLIED TO THIS COMPANY BEFORE? ☐ YES ☐ NO	WHERE?	WHEN?

Education History

NAME & LOCATION OF SCHOOL	YEARS ATTENDED	DID YOU GRADUATE?	SUBJECTS STUDIED
GRAMMAR SCHOOL			
HIGH SCHOOL			
COLLEGE			
TRADE, BUSINESS OR CORRESPONDENCE SCHOOL			

General Information

SUBJECTS OF SPECIAL STUDY/ RESEARCH WORK OR SPECIAL TRAINING/SKILLS	
U.S. MILITARY OR NAVAL SERVICE	RANK

Former Employers
LIST LAST THREE EMPLOYERS, STARTING WITH LAST ONE FIRST

DATE MONTH & YEAR	NAME & ADDRESS OF EMPLOYER	SALARY	POSITION	REASON FOR LEAVING

References
GIVE BELOW THE NAMES OF THREE PERSONS NOT RELATED TO YOU, WHOM HAVE KNOWN YOU ONE YEAR

NAME	ADDRESS	BUSINESS

Be prepared to supply all the information required on this sample form.

Surviving the Job Interview

After you fill out the application, you should prepare for the interview. When applying for a job at a restaurant, be as knowledgeable as possible about that restaurant. If possible, eat at the restaurant before you fill out your application. This will give you a great advantage.

You will have insight into the restaurant's menu, service, and clientele. It makes a great impression during an interview if you can knowledgeably speak about the restaurant and the experience it is attempting to provide for guests.

A good interviewer will ask you very broad and open questions designed to give you an opportunity to sell yourself. Take full advantage of these opportunities. Some questions may seem odd to you, and you might not understand what they have to do with waiting tables. Play the game. The interviewer may be trying to see how quickly you can think on your feet. Make sure you mention how well you can anticipate customer needs and how good you are at the art of selling. Communicate to the interviewer how much pride you take in your work and in your job performance. Don't just say you like people. Say you like people and you like waiting tables.

Remember, if you cannot sell yourself, then how can you sell food and wine? Also, some interviewer change subjects often during an interview to see if applicants can think quickly and not be rattled. Do your best to answer any question cheerfully and with a positive response.

The interviewer will probably ask when you are available to work. Do not tell him or her that you would prefer to have certain days off. You are applying for work, and you should be ready and willing to work when your employer needs you. However, if you have schedule conflicts such as school, mention those.

The interviewer may also ask if you would mind performing a different job than the one you are applying for on a temporary basis. If possible, you should agree. This will show that you are flexible and have a , helpful attitude. After all, the goal is to get the job!

Each interviewer looks for different things in an applicant. Some of the questions that interviewers may ask themselves during an interview include the following:

- Does this person have a sense of style?
- Does this person carry himself/herself well?

- Is this person a restaurant person?
- Do I trust this person to talk to my guests?
- Will this person work well with my staff?
- Can this person add to my restaurant's reputation for service?

Come prepared with a question or two to ask the interviewer. A thoughtful question will show the interviewer that you are serious about your application and have thought about the business. Some good questions to ask could include: How do you handle guest complaints? What kind of ongoing training do you offer? Do you offer health insurance? What are the opportunities for advancement?

Keeping your job

Once you have been offered and have accepted a job, you will begin training. Make sure that you report to work in the proper uniform and with the proper equipment—pens, wine tool, crumber, and so on—if your restaurant does not supply these items to you.

To get the most out of your training, observe the following rules:

- Pay close attention and take notes if you need to.
- Ask questions.
- Listen to what is said. Listen with your whole body. Absorb as much information as you can in the quickest amount of time.
- Show a willingness to work and to be a part of the team.
- Be kind and polite.
- Make a great first impression on everyone you meet.
- Smile. Look as if you are happy to be there.
- It is okay to be nervous, but be confident that your skills and abilities will enable you to master the job.
- Do not criticize the way things are done. Things are done a certain way for a reason. Eventually, you will learn the reason.

- Never compare your new job to your old job. Hearing that another restaurant does something better is not going to sit well with your new coworkers.
- Ask for feedback. Ask your coworkers and your manager how you are doing.

You will most likely be paid minimum wage during training, and should not expect tips. That is how the system usually works. Your day to train the new person and have him or her do your work and give you the tips will come. The most important thing to remember about training is this: You must prove yourself. You must also:

- Show your managers and coworkers that you are a good hire and that you are not afraid of hard work.
- Quickly become part of the team.
- Do your homework and memorize the menus and ingredients.
- Quickly become familiar with everything the restaurant has to offer its guests.

The more you know, the more you sell. The more you sell, the more you earn. The more you earn, the more money the restaurant makes. This will make you a happy and successful wait person, and will make your manager happy that you were hired. As you gain experience waiting tables, you will want to keep developing new service skills and techniques to make your job easier and more lucrative. The waiting game is always changing—you must always keep developing new techniques. The best ways to do this are through continued on-the-job training and real-life experience.

On-the-Job Training

Waiting tables is not an assembly-line type of job. It is a people-to-people job. To win the waiting game, you have to combine the skills of an actor, a psychologist, and sometimes even a doctor. No two tables are the same. Each table presents a new situation and a new set of people. The more on-the-job experience you have, the better you will be able to deliver service that suits the needs of each of your guests.

Real-Life Experience

To learn about service, all you have to do is look around. Seventy-five percent of the U.S. economy is service related. Sit up and pay attention to the people who serve you. How do you like to be treated? How does it feel when you're ignored? Do you want to do business with someone who delivers bad service? Learn from the successes and mistakes of the people who serve you every day.

The next time you go to a mall, spend an hour observing the service going on around you. Watch for things like:

- Greetings: Did the server at the coffee shop smile when guests approached?
- Appearance: Did the look of the clerks at the clothing store make you want to buy?
- Attitude: Did you have to ask for help?

Make a list of ten great service techniques that you notice. Talk about them with your friends. Remember, there is no better way to understand service than to look at it from the guest's perspective.

Congratulations! You have just completed the essential guide to waiting tables. You are well on your way to winning the waiting game and starting a great career in the restaurant industry. If you have any questions or comments, write us at The Waiting Game, P.O. Box 1548, Austin, TX 78767-1548.

GLOSSARY

86: A menu item that is temporarily unavailable. For example, "86 poached salmon." Most restaurants have a board listing 86ed items. No one is quite sure where this term came from. Two suggestions: Depression-era soup pots held 85 cups of soup, and when the pot was empty, the server called out "86 soup"; a popular Chicago train line had 86 as its final stop. *86ed* can also mean that a guest has been ejected. *68ed* means that a menu item has become available.

Ace: A single guest at a table.

À la carte: A menu item that is sold as a separate dish and is priced separately. À la carte service is different from *prix fixe*, in which entire meals are sold for one price.

Aging: For beef, the process of refrigeration for a specific amount of time to optimize tenderness and flavor. For wine, the process of storing in oak or steel barrels to add flavor.

All day: Used by cooks referring to current orders. For example, "I need seven orders of french fries all day."

American service: Restaurant service in which individual orders are prepared in the kitchen, put on plates, and served to guests by a wait person.

Appetizer: A small portion of food served at the beginning of a meal to awaken the appetite.

Arm service: Carrying and serving dishes and beverages without using a tray.

Atmosphere: The tone set by the décor of a restaurant.

B & B: A small plate for bread and butter.

Back (water or beer): A glass of water or beer served along with a cocktail.

Back of the house (BOH): The kitchen.

Banquet: A dinner in honor of some person or occasion.

Bar back: The assistant to the bartender.

Bartender: The person in charge of preparing cocktails.

Beef: Meat from cattle (see page 111).

Beer: An alcoholic beverage made from germinated barley, hops, and yeast (see page 71).

Bottom line: The profit earned by a restaurant.

Brand loyal: A guest who prefers one brand of alcoholic beverage to any other brand.

Breakdown: The job of closing the kitchen, putting away all food, and scrubbing down the entire kitchen.

Breathe: The process that allows wine to achieve its full flavor when a wine bottle is opened and exposed to the air.

Bus person: A wait person's helper. Also called a *busser.*

Bussing: Clearing a table.

Call brand: A premium brand of liquor, usually better quality and more expensive than a *well brand.*

Caterer: A person who provides food and services for an event.

Chafing dish: A two-part dish with a heat source under it for cooking and serving food. The upper part of the dish contains the food, the lower part contains water.

Chair order: A system for keeping track of orders, in which every chair at a table is given a particular number.

Champagne: A type of sparkling wine produced in Champagne, France.

Check: A guest's bill.

Check presenter: A folder in which the check is presented to the guest.

Glossary

Cheese board: A serving platter used to display an array of cheeses. The phrase refers both to the platter and the presentation itself.

Chef: The person in charge of all kitchen activities. In large kitchens, a *head chef* or *executive chef* is the person in charge of all kitchen activities.

Chief executive officer (CEO): An officer of a corporation. If a corporation owns the restaurant, the CEO may also work as the general manager of the restaurant.

Chit: *See* Dupe.

Clearing: Removing service items from a table.

Clientele: Regular guests.

Closure: The end of the dining experience.

Cocktail tray: *See* Drink tray.

Cocktail: A mixed drink of alcohol and other ingredients (see page 74). Also called a *mixed drink*.

Condiment: A seasoning.

Corkage: The fee paid for opening and serving a bottle of wine by a guest who brings a bottle of wine to a restaurant.

Corked: Wine that has spoiled due to a faulty cork.

Cover: A single guest or a single place setting.

Covers: The number of guests served during a particular shift.

Cross-contamination: The transfer of germs from one object or food to another.

Crumber: A device used to clear bread crumbs and food debris from the table (see illustration, page 47).

Cut off (a guest): Refuse alcoholic beverage service to a guest.

Decant: To pour a bottle of wine into a carafe or other container in order to let the wine breathe.

Demitasse [DEHM-ee-tass]: A small cup for serving espresso.

Dessert menu: A menu that lists just desserts.

Dessert tray: A tray or cart on which sample desserts are displayed.

Deuce: A table for two guests. Also called a *two top*.

Dine and dash: A guest who leaves without paying.

Dishwasher: A restaurant employee who washes dishes.

Draught (draft) beer: Beer that is served from a keg rather than a bottle or can.

Drink tray: A small, round tray for carrying cocktails or drinks (see page 44). Also called a *cocktail tray*.

Drop: to present, or serve, something to a table.

Dupe: A duplicate of an order. Also called a *chit*.

Entrée: The main course of a meal.

Expediter: A person stationed in the kitchen who is in charge of coordinating interaction between the kitchen and the front of the house.

Finger bowl: A small bowl partially filled with water in which guests rinse their fingers after eating messy foods.

Firing: To start cooking a particular order.

First in, first out (FIFO): A method of food storage in which foods that go into a storage area first are also brought out first.

Flatware: Another term for silverware.

Food allergy: A condition in which someone becomes sick if he or she eats a certain type of food.

Food poisoning: An illness caused by eating spoiled or contaminated food.

Food runner: A staff member who delivers orders to the wait person or directly to the table.

Food tray: *See* Service tray.

Four top: A table for four guests.

French service: Restaurant service in which individual orders are prepared by the wait person at the side of the table (see illustration, page 5).

Front of the house (FOH): The dining room.

Full-service restaurant: A restaurant in which guests sit down and order from a menu, as opposed to a fast-food or cafeteria-style restaurant.

Grades of beef: Different qualities of beef. *Prime* is the highest quality, *choice* is the second highest, and *select* is the third highest.

Grill cook: A line cook who specializes in grilling foods.

Halal: Food that is approved for consumption by Muslims.

Head: The foam on a glass of beer.

Host: The restaurant staff person who is responsible for seating guests.

Hotel tray: *See* Service tray.

House: Restaurant (see illustration, page 8).

In the weeds: Having more to do than humanly possible. Also referred to as *weeded*, meaning too busy to ask for help.

Kosher: Foods that are approved for consumption by Jews.

Lactose intolerance: The inability to digest lactose, also known as milk sugar. Lactose-intolerant individuals experience an upset stomach when they consume milk or milk-based foods.

Liability: Being legally bound to compensate someone for an injury.

Line: The stations in the kitchen where the chef and his crew work. The grill, stoves, fryers, and pantry are usually located on the line.

Line cooks: Cooks who work in the section of the kitchen known as the line.

Linen: A term used to refer to all table accessories made from cloth.

Liqueur: A strong, sweet alcoholic beverage, usually served as an after-dinner drink.

Liquor: A distilled alcoholic beverage (see chapter 6, Alcoholic Beverage Service).

Lowboy: A refrigerator under a counter.

Maître d' (maître d'hôtel): The manager of the dining room.

Marking a table: Placing the correct silverware on a table prior to serving a course.

Meal policy: A restaurant's policy concerning employees eating at the restaurant.

Menu: The list of dishes and beverages offered for sale by a restaurant.

Mixed drink: *See* Cocktail.

No-show: A guest who doesn't show up for a reservation.

On point: Proper alignment of tables and table settings in a section.

On the fly: Needed immediately, for example, "One veal cutlet, on the fly."

On the rocks: A beverage served with ice.

On the side: Serving a food item separately, for example, "Salad dressing, on the side."

Pantry: The section of the kitchen in which the cold items are prepared.

Payroll: The salaries paid to a restaurant's employees. Also called *staff costs*.

Pepper mill: A pepper grinder.

Pick up: Telling the kitchen that a table is ready for the next course, for example, "Pick up on table 24."

Pilferage: Theft of items from a restaurant by the staff.

Place setting: *See* Table setting.

Plate: To arrange foods on a plate for serving.

Plate covers: Metal covers placed over plates to protect the food being served.

Platter: A large, shallow dish used to serve food.

Point-of-sale (POS) system: A computerized ordering system.

Pre-bussing: Clearing off certain plates and glasses during the course of a meal.

Premium brand: A high-quality brand of liquor.

Prep: To prepare food for cooking, as in chopping vegetables, washing lettuce, and so on.

Prep cooks: Cooks who help prepare the food for cooking.

Prime costs: A restaurant's food and beverage costs plus payroll costs.

Prix fixe [PREE FEEKS]: A complete meal offered at a fixed price, in contrast to *à la carte* service, in which different menu items are sold individually at different prices.

Profit: The money a restaurant retains after paying prime costs and associated expenses. The average restaurant in the United States makes a profit of 4 percent.

Proof: The alcohol content of alcoholic beverages.

Reach-in: A refrigeration unit that is reached into, as opposed to a *walk-in*, a refrigeration unit that is walked into.

Reading the table: Figuring out what kind of attention the guests at a particular table require.

Restaurant limit: The maximum number of alcoholic beverages a restaurant will serve a guest before the guest is *cut off*, or not served any more alcoholic beverages.

Roll-up: Silverware rolled into a napkin.

Runner: The staff member who brings the food from the kitchen to the table.

Russian service: Restaurant service in which the wait person brings out a large platter of food and serves portions to guests at the table (see illustration, page 6).

Sauceboat: A china or silver container for sauces served alongside food.

Sauté cook: A cook who specializes in sauté cooking.

Section: The part of the restaurant in which a wait person's tables are located.

Server: Another term for a *wait person*.

Service napkins: Napkins used for handling hot plates and for serving wine and champagne.

Service plate: A plate with a folded napkin on which fresh silverware is brought to the table. Also called *STP (service transport plate)*.

Service tray: A large, oval tray used for carrying dishes (see page 42). Also called a *food tray* or *hotel tray*.

Setups: The items needed for a table setting, including silverware and glassware.

Shift: The period of time a wait person is scheduled to work.

Show plate: A plate set in the center of a table for decorative interest.

Side stand: A station used to store items that a wait person needs.

Side towel: A folded napkin used as a serving tool.

Side work: Work needed to prepare a restaurant before the arrival of guests.

Slammed: Almost too busy to get the job done.

Sommelier [so-mel-YAY]: A wine steward in a restaurant.

SOS: Abbreviation for "sauce on the side."

Sous-chef: The chef immediately under the head chef.

Sparkling wine: A bubbly wine, like champagne.

Staff costs: *See* Payroll.

Steep: To put a tea bag or loose tea in a hot water for a few minutes to draw the tea from the tea leaves.

Stemware: Glassware with a stem.

Stiff: To depart a restaurant without tipping the wait staff.

STP (service transport plate): *See* Service plate.

Table maintenance: Discreetly removing used plates, silverware, and debris as necessary during the course of the meal. Includes pre-bussing and refreshing silverware.

Table setting: The proper arrangement of silverware, plates, glasses, and other items on a table (see illustration, page 23). Refers both to the group of objects as well as to the act of placing them. Also called a *place setting*.

Tapas [TAH-pahs]: Appetizers or food served on small plates, in Spanish cuisine.

Tea caddy: A set of pots on a small tray for tea service.

Tip: The money paid by a guest to a wait person in excess of the food and beverage charges.

Tip out: The act of sharing tips with coworkers.

Tip report: The record of all tips maintained by a wait person for tax purposes.

Tray jack: A stand used for supporting a service tray (see illustration, page 43). Also called a *tray stand*.

Tray stand: *See* Tray jack.

Two top: A table for two guests. Also called a *deuce*.

Underliner: A large plate, used in serving, on which to place a bowl of soup or other food.

Varietals: Wines identified by the variety of grape they are made from.

Vegan: A person who avoids all animal products, including eggs, dairy products, and honey.

Vegetarian: A person who avoids eating meat.

Vintage: The year in which the grapes for a particular wine were grown and picked.

Wait staff: The restaurant employees primarily responsible for taking food orders and serving food and beverage items.

Waiter station: A wait person's section, or the location of his or her side stand.

Walk the check: To leave a restaurant without paying the check.

Walk-in: A refrigeration unit large enough to walk into. It can also mean a guest without a reservation.

Weeded: *See* In the weeds.

Well brand: The brand of liquor poured when a guest does not specify a brand, usually less expensive and of poorer quality than a *call brand*.

Well liquor: The brand of liquor served by a bartender if the guest does not ask for a particular brand.

Whiskey: An alcoholic beverage distilled from mashed grain and aged in charred oak barrels (see page 75). The alternate spelling, *whisky*, refers to Scotch, Irish, and Canadian.

Wine: Fermented grape juice (see chapter 7, All About Wine).

Wine list: A menu of wines offered by a restaurant (see illustration, pages 93 and 94).

Wine tool: A tool used to open wines (see illustrations, page 101).

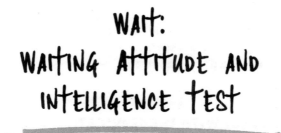

WAIT:
WAITING ATTITUDE AND
INTELLIGENCE TEST

Now that you have read and studied *The Waiting Game,* it's time for you to test your knowledge. Answer the following questions as best as you can. After you understand them all, you are well on your way to success in the waiting game.

1. Restaurants control what three important factors in determining the quality of a guest's dining experience:

    _____

    _____

    _____

MATCH THE DEFINITION WITH THE APPROPRIATE TERM

2. Restaurant service in which the wait person brings out a large platter of food and serves portions to guests at the table ____

3. Restaurant service in which orders are prepared by the wait person at the side of the table ____

4. Restaurant service in which individual orders are prepared in the kitchen, put on plates, and served to guests by a wait person ____

A. American service
B. Russian service
C. French service

MATCH THE GUEST WITH THE SERVICE THEY MIGHT WANT

5. Businesspeople ____
6. Tourists ____
7. Couples ____

A. Informal and chatty
B. Invisible
C. Formal and businesslike

MATCH THE DEFINITION WITH THE APPROPRIATE TERM

8. Proper alignment of tables and table settings in a section ____

9. Being so busy that it is difficult to deliver proper service ____

10. Figuring out what kind of attention the guests at a particular table require ____

11. The part of the restaurant in which a wait person's tables are located ____

A. Read the table
B. In the weeds
C. Section
D. On point

MATCH THE DEFINITION WITH THE APPROPRIATE TERM

12. The brand of liquor poured
when a guest does not specify
a brand, usually less expensive
and of lesser quality than a call
brand _____

A. Brand loyal
B. Well brand
C. Premium brand
D. 86ed

13. A dish that is temporarily
unavailable _____

14. A guest who prefers one brand of
alcoholic beverage to others _____

15. A higher quality brand of
liquor _____

FILL IN THE BLANKS

16. Serve women _____.

17. Serve food from the _____ side of the guest.

18. Serve beverages from the _____ side of the guest.

19. Remove plates and glasses from the _____ side of the guest.

20. Respect your guests' personal _____.

21. LL RR means "lower _____, raise _____."

22. Most restaurants offer the courses of a meal in what order?

1._____

2._____

3._____

4._____

MATCH THE DEFINITION WITH THE APPROPRIATE TERM

23. Espresso mixed with a large amount of steamed milk and topped with a little foamed milk _____

24. Espresso mixed with a little steamed milk and topped with foamed milk _____

25. Coffee brewed by forcing hot water through finely ground coffee beans _____

A. Espresso
B. Cappuccino
C. Caffè latte

MATCH THE DEFINITION WITH THE APPROPRIATE TERM

26. A plate used to help serve a bowl of soup or other food _____

27. Discreetly removing used plates, silverware, and debris as necessary during the course of the meal _____

28. A metal device used to clear bread crumbs and food debris from the table

29. A folded napkin used as a serving tool _____

A. Crumber
B. Underliner
C. Side towel
D. Table maintenance

30. What are four benefits of using trays?

_____

_____

_____

_____

MATCH THE DEFINITION WITH THE APPROPRIATE TERM

31. A stand used for supporting a service tray _____

32. Carrying and serving dishes and beverages without using a tray _____

33. Clearing a table _____

A. Bussing
B. Arm service
C. Tray jack

FILL IN THE BLANKS

34. Never _____ with an angry guest.

35. If a guest complains, _____ sincerely.

36. View complaints as valuable pieces of _____.

37. If you feel that a guest is being abusive to you, you should

_____.

MATCH THE DEFINITION WITH THE APPROPRIATE TERM

38. The transfer of germs from one item or food to another ____
A. Food poisoning
B. Cross-contamination
C. FIFO

39. A method of food storage in which foods that go into a storage area first are also brought out first ____

40. An illness caused by eating spoiled or contaminated food ____

MATCH THE DEFINITION WITH THE APPROPRIATE TERM

41. A folder in which the check is presented to the guest ____
A. Check presenter
B. Closure

42. The end of the dining experience ____

FILL IN THE BLANKS

43. For every dollar the restaurant makes in sales, it keeps about _____ cents.

44. Pilferage is _____.

45. You have to pay income _____ based on your hourly wage plus tips.

MATCH THE DEFINITION WITH THE APPROPRIATE TERM

46. The act of sharing tips with coworkers ____

47. Theft of items from a restaurant by the staff ____

48. The profit earned by a restaurant ____

A. Pilferage

B. Bottom line

C. Tip out

49. A restaurant is divided into what three sections?

_____

_____

_____

MATCH THE DEFINITION WITH THE APPROPRIATE TERM

50. The person in charge of all activities in the dining room ____

51. A wine manager in a restaurant ____

52. The person in charge of all the kitchen activities ____

A. Sommelier

B. Maître d'

C. Chef

MATCH THE DEFINITION WITH THE APPROPRIATE TERM

53. An alcoholic beverage made from germinated barley, hops, and yeast ____

54. A beverage served with ice ____

55. A distilled alcoholic beverage ____

A. Liquor

B. Beer

C. On the rocks

56. Servers should be able to answer what three questions about the various wines offered by the restaurant?

_____

_____

_____

MATCH THE DEFINITION WITH THE APPROPRIATE TERM

57. Wine that has spoiled due to a faulty cork ____

58. The year in which the grapes for a particular wine were grown and picked ____

59. A bubbly wine, like champagne ____

A. Sparkling wine

B. Vintage

C. Corked

FILL IN THE BLANKS

60. Veal is a meat that comes from _____.

61. Salmon is a _____ water fish.

62. Trout is a _____ water fish.

63. Mushrooms are actually not a vegetable, but a _____.

TRUE OR FALSE?

64. Lobsters are crustaceans. _____

65. Bok choy is a cephalopod. _____

MATCH THE DEFINITION WITH THE APPROPRIATE TERM

66. Boneless cuts of fish or meat ____

67. Foods that are permissible for consumption according to the Jewish dietary laws ____

68. A person who avoids all animal products, including eggs, dairy products, and honey ____

A. Kosher foods

B. Vegan

C. Fillet

Once you have finished taking the **W**aiting **A**ttitude and Intelligence **T**est, check your answers against those listed below.

1. Service, atmosphere, and food **2.** B **3.** C **4.** A **5.** C **6.** A **7.** B **8.** D **9.** B **10.** A **11.** C **12.** B **13.** D **14.** A **15.** C **16.** First **17.** Left **18.** Right **19.** Right **20.** Space **21.** Left, right **22.** Appetizers, soup, salad, and entrées **23.** B **24.** C **25.** A **26.** B **27.** D **28.** A **29.** C **30.** Better serving efficiency, better serving style, better control over spills and other accidents, and better sanitation **31.** C **32.** B **33.** A **34.** Argue **35.** Apologize **36.** Information **37.** Tell your manager **38.** B **39.** C **40.** A **41.** A **42.** B **43.** 4 cents **44.** Theft **45.** Tax **46.** C **47.** A **48.** B **49.** The owners or CEOS, the front of the house (dining room), and the back of the house (kitchen) **50.** B **51.** A **52.** C **53.** B **54.** C **55.** A **56.** What does it taste like? Is it a good value? What foods go with it? **57.** C **58.** B **59.** A **60.** Cattle **61.** Salt **62.** Fresh **63.** Fungus **64.** True **65.** False **66.** C **67.** A **68.** B

SELECTED BIBLIOGRAPHY

Aikin, Brenton R. *The Waiter/Waitress Manual.* New York: McGraw-Hill, 1976.

Bittman, Mark. *How to Cook Everything: Simple Recipes for Great Food.* New York: Macmillan, 1998.

Clarke, Oz. *Oz Clarke's New Encyclopedia of Wine.* London: Webster's International Publishers Limited, 1999.

The Culinary Institute of America. *Remarkable Service.* New York: John Wiley & Sons, 2001.

Dahmer, Sondra J., and Kurt W. Kohl. *The Waiter and Waitress Training Manual,* 4th ed. New York: John Wiley & Sons, 1995.

Davidson, Alan. *The Oxford Companion to Food.* Oxford (England) and New York: Oxford University Press, 1999.

École Technique Hotelière Tsuji. *Professional Restaurant Service.* New York: John Wiley & Sons, 1991.

Hoving, Walter. *Tiffany's Table Manners for Teenagers.* New York: Random House, 1989.

Julyan, Brian K. *Sales and Service for the Wine Professional.* London and New York: Cassell, 1999.

Katsigris, Costas, and Mary Porter. *The Bar and Beverage Book: Basics of Profitable Management.* New York: John Wiley & Sons, 1983.

McCarthy, Ed, et al. *Wine for Dummies*. New York: Hungry Minds Inc., 1998.

Plotkin, Robert. *The Bartender's Companion: A Complete Drink Recipe Guide,* 3rd ed. Tucson: R. Plotkin Barmedia, 1997.

Strianese, Anthony J. *Dining Room and Banquet Management,* 2nd ed. Albany, New York: Delmar Publishing, 1997.

Zraly, Kevin. *Windows on the World Complete Wine Course*. New York: Sterling Publishing, 1999.

INDEX

About the Authors

Mike Kirkham has been winning the waiting game since 1979, when he started waiting tables in Corpus Christi at age seventeen. Mike served, cleaned, and tended bar at a number of restaurants and hotels in Texas until 1989, when he went to work for Peggy Weiss at the Shoreline Grill, a fine-dining waterfront restaurant in downtown Austin. By 1993, he was managing the Shoreline and was key in making the restaurant a success. Mike's seen it all in the business: bad service and good service; booze, drugs, and theft; culinary triumphs and dining disasters. His wide range of experience as a manager and trainer forms the heart of *The Waiting Game*.

Peggy Weiss knows service talent when she sees it. Born and raised in New Iberia, Louisiana, Peggy is a founding partner in Austin's Jeffrey's Restaurant, a nationally acclaimed culinary landmark. Rated as the top restaurant in Austin by *Texas Monthly* magazine, Jeffrey's continues to rack up record sales and capture numerous industry awards. In addition to helping build Jeffrey's, Peggy is an owner of the Shoreline Grill in downtown Austin; Cipollina, an Italian takeout cafe in

Austin; and Jeffrey's, at the Watergate in Washington, D.C. Even though she is a consummate professional, Peggy is not strictly business. She dedicates her enthusiasm and her success to helping others, serving as a board member for Share Our Strength, an organization dedicated to hunger relief in Texas, and as a committee chair for Laura Bush's Texas Book Festival, dedicated to raising money for Texas public libraries. Peggy, along with her husband, Ron, received the Who's Who in Wine and Food in Texas Award for 2001. *Nation's Restaurant News* inducted Jeffrey's into the Fine Dining Hall of Fame for 2002.

Bill Crawford is a best-selling author, an award-winning journalist, and a longtime observer of the American cultural scene. His work has appeared in *Texas Monthly, American Way, Oklahoma Today,* and numerous other publications. He is the coauthor of more than a dozen books, including *Stevie Ray Vaughan: Caught in the Crossfire* (Little, Brown, 1993), *Cerealizing America: The Unsweetened Story of American Breakfast Cereal* (Faber & Faber, 1995), and *Austin: An Illustrated History* (American Historical Press, 2001). Crawford lives in Austin, Texas, and is trying desperately to teach his kids how to win the waiting game so that they can pay their way through college.